Joan of Arc

A Captivating Guide to a Heroine of France and Her Role During the Lancastrian Phase of the Hundred Years' War

© **Copyright 2019**

All Rights Reserved. No part of this book may be reproduced in any form without permission in writing from the author. Reviewers may quote brief passages in reviews.

Disclaimer: No part of this publication may be reproduced or transmitted in any form or by any means, mechanical or electronic, including photocopying or recording, or by any information storage and retrieval system, or transmitted by email without permission in writing from the publisher.

While all attempts have been made to verify the information provided in this publication, neither the author nor the publisher assumes any responsibility for errors, omissions or contrary interpretations of the subject matter herein.

This book is for entertainment purposes only. The views expressed are those of the author alone, and should not be taken as expert instruction or commands. The reader is responsible for his or her own actions.

Adherence to all applicable laws and regulations, including international, federal, state and local laws governing professional licensing, business practices, advertising and all other aspects of doing business in the US, Canada, UK or any other jurisdiction is the sole responsibility of the purchaser or reader.

Neither the author nor the publisher assumes any responsibility or liability whatsoever on the behalf of the purchaser or reader of these materials. Any perceived slight of any individual or organization is purely unintentional.

Free Bonus from Captivating History (Available for a Limited time)

Hi History Lovers!

Now you have a chance to join our exclusive history list so you can get your first history ebook for free as well as discounts and a potential to get more history books for free! Simply visit the link below to join.

Captivatinghistory.com/ebook

Also, make sure to follow us on Facebook, Twitter and Youtube by searching for Captivating History.

Contents

INTRODUCTION 1

CHAPTER 1 – THE UNENDING WAR 3

CHAPTER 2 – A WHISPERED PROPHECY 8

CHAPTER 3 – THE FIRST VISION 14

CHAPTER 4 – THE DOUBT OF BAUDRICOURT 19

CHAPTER 5 – A PREDICTION OF DEFEAT 25

CHAPTER 6 – AN AUDIENCE WITH THE KING 31

CHAPTER 7 – THE ROAD TO ORLÉANS 36

CHAPTER 8 – ARRIVAL AT ORLÉANS 41

CHAPTER 9 – FLYING THE WHITE BANNER 45

CHAPTER 10 – A SIGN PROVIDED 50

CHAPTER 11 – THE BATTLE OF PATAY..55

CHAPTER 12 – BEANS FOR THE APOCALYPSE..60

CHAPTER 13 – THE FRENCH KING CROWNED...66

CHAPTER 14 – THE SIEGE OF PARIS...70

CHAPTER 15 – PEACE..75

CHAPTER 16 – CAPTURE 79

CHAPTER 17 – CAPTIVE 84

CHAPTER 18 – A SAINT TRIED FOR HERESY...89

CHAPTER 19 – THE BURNING OF JEANNE D'ARC...94

CONCLUSION..97

SOURCES 104

Introduction

Joan of Arc. Some see her as a lunatic; some, as a sadly misunderstood piece of history; others, as a power-hungry genius; and the Catholic Church, as a saint and a symbol of faith, humility, and courage in the face of persecution. Yet one thing cannot be denied: Joan of Arc was one of the most remarkable figures in the story of the human race, and her extraordinary life is a fascinating tale that leaves many questions unanswered by history.

When Joan arrived on the scene, France was a country in dire straits. Almost completely defeated by the English, it was on the very brink of becoming little more than a jewel in the English crown. The rightful heir to its throne, the Dauphin Charles, was a dispirited and morose man who had given up on ever ruling his country. The time had never been more ripe for a savior, and yet no savior had ever been as unlikely as Joan. She was no warrior, nor was she a princess, nor was she educated in any way. Instead, she was just a peasant and a woman besides. In the medieval era, such a person was of practically no consequence.

Except Joan didn't let that stop her. Inspired by what she believed to be divine revelation, she dared to demand an audience with the Dauphin, even though she was of the lowest birth imaginable. She might not have been able to read or write, yet she was determined to save her country. It has been said that faith can move mountains. It is difficult to imagine a bigger mountain than the one that the faith of Joan moved.

Joan's story almost feels like a novel instead of a part of history. She was a shining savior on a warhorse, waving her white banner and calling her soldiers forth to victory; but she was also painfully and intensely human, a young girl who wept and bled just the same as the rest of us. In the same breath, it is as easy to relate to Joan as it is to be awed by her incredible character. She may have been beatified as a saint, but Joan of Arc was in many ways a very ordinary human being, a person who felt pain and fear, a person who made mistakes and who had moments of weakness. This book follows her through her extraordinary journey. Feel her terror as she first experienced her visions. See her determination as she convinced a cynical captain to grant her passage to the Dauphin. Experience her exhilaration and faith as she led the French army to victory after victory. Weep alongside her as the King of France betrayed her. Suffer with her during her long imprisonment in the hands of her enemies. And cry with the witnesses who saw her burn for a crime she did not commit.

She was Joan of Arc, a person whose life remains wreathed in mystery, but nonetheless a fascinating adventure. And this is her story.

Chapter 1 – The Unending War

It all started with a baby—a baby girl, to be exact. If the tiny, newborn Blanche of France, born on April 1st, 1328, had just come into the world as a bouncing baby boy instead of a little girl, then the war might never have started. It was a twisted thing that such a small kink of fate should have the capacity to cause such widespread and enduring tragedy—and if it was not for the sexist laws of the era, as there would have been no conflict over the throne of France. Yet Blanche, the youngest of King Charles IV's two surviving daughters, happened to be born in a time when a woman was not allowed to rule the kingdom of France. And so, it was declared that Blanche's late father had died without an heir. The Capetian dynasty ended with him.

King Charles IV was the youngest surviving son of Philip IV, who had three boys. Each had been king in his turn after Philip's death: first Louis X, then Philip V, and then, finally, Charles. The only other siblings that were left were an older sister, Margaret, and a younger one, Isabella. Charles's younger brother Robert had died as a boy. Again because of their gender, neither of the women could take the throne. But perhaps Isabella could provide an heir—an heir that would be most unsatisfying to the French nobility. In a bid to improve diplomatic relations between France and England, Isabella had been married off to the prince of England when she was only twelve years old. But now she was a grown woman in her thirties, a fiercely intelligent one who had earned the title of She-Wolf of France, and her husband was the teenaged King Edward II of England. As the closest male relative of the late king of France, Edward had a legitimate claim to the French throne.

The French nobility scrambled to prevent the unthinkable of one man being the king of both France and England. They managed to come up with an alternative heir. Philip of Valois had been a fairly minor noble as the son of a count; much of his life prior to the death of King Charles IV has been lost to history as he was not considered important during his childhood. But his father, while a minor noble, was also the youngest brother of Philip IV—Charles IV's father—which made Philip of Valois the closest relative to the deceased king through the male line. He was hurriedly crowned King Philip VI of France before Edward could lay claim to the throne.

To rub salt in the wound, Edward was not only King of England but also Duke of Aquitaine—a large duchy in France—due to the fact that the kings of England had long owed their heritage to French blood since William the Conqueror's victories in 1066. For that reason, Edward was also technically a vassal of the king of France, which forced him to pay homage to the king. Paying homage was a humiliating ceremony that involved swearing allegiance and showing submission, and Edward did not intend to pay homage to a king that he believed had stolen his second throne.

Isabella had been married off to Edward in an attempt to make peace. In a horrible twist of fate, that very act ended up sparking the longest conflict in European history. It didn't take long for Edward, a hotheaded teenager, to violate the homage ceremony by wearing his sword and crown instead of being bareheaded as was custom. In retaliation, Philip attempted to confiscate Aquitaine. Edward accepted the challenge by forcing his claim to the French throne. In 1337, the call to arms was sounded. It was war.

* * * *

The Hundred Years' War has since become known as one of the longest conflicts in the history of the world. Up until World War I claimed that title, it was also known as the Great War. Starting in 1337, it would remain primarily a conflict over succession, raging between the English Plantagenet family and the French House of Valois. The amount of vitriol and combat that the war entailed eventually overflowed into several proxy wars, including the War of the Breton Succession and the Castilian Civil War, during which France and England would each pick a side and lend support to whichever champion they had chosen.

The first major battle, the Battle of Sluys in 1340, was a naval battle which was decisively won by the English, allowing them to invade France and lay siege to the fortress of Tournai. France fought back, attacking England on three fronts: in France itself, along the English coastline by burning and plundering several cities, and from the Scottish border via one of the most important French allies—King David I of Scotland.

However, as the first phase of the war stretched into the decades, England started to seize the upper hand. The English won the Battle of Crécy using the prowess of common longbowmen to defeat the magnificent French cavalry, an ignominious defeat for the haughty French. This was followed by more English victories at Neville's Cross and Calais, and then, finally—after a brief interlude while both countries were occupied with facing the Black Plague—Poitiers. This last victory resulted in the capture of the French king, Philip VI's successor John II. John was shipped back to England and ransomed for a ridiculous sum of money.

In 1360, King Edward led another campaign through crippled France. The country was struggling under its young leader, the Dauphin Charles, whose efforts were focused on taxing the peasants in order to be able to pay his father's ransom. Edward swept across the country, heading for Reims and Paris, two of France's most important cities. But Black Monday put a stop to all of that. A freak hailstorm broke out above Edward's troops, killing several thousand men and horses. Edward took this as a sign from God that this campaign was against His will and returned to England, resulting in the first treaty of the war. The Treaty of Brétigny renounced Edward's claim to the throne but restored Aquitaine to his possession. King Edward returned to England, leaving his son, Edward the Black Prince, in charge of Aquitaine.

The peace did not last long. The second phase of the war (known as the Caroline War) began only nine years later. The Black Prince's involvement in the Castilian Civil War had left him physically ill and financially crippled, forcing him to heavily tax his subjects in Aquitaine. King Edward III was getting old and sick himself, and King John II had finally died in captivity. His son was crowned Charles V. When some of the Black Prince's nobles from Aquitaine appealed to King Charles for help, the French king was delighted. He extended a polite summons to the Black Prince requesting his presence at France, whereupon the Prince declared that he would be there—with an invading army. All-out war began again.

This time, the French had the upper hand. With England's two most important military leaders incapacitated by age and illness, France was led by an angry king who had been waiting for this opportunity for far too long. By 1372, several territories were back under French control, including Poitiers and the important port town of La Rochelle. Raids by Englishmen John of Gaunt and the Earl of Buckingham proved ineffective as the French continued to recapture their lost ground.

When the Black Prince, King Edward, and King Charles died in 1376, 1377, and 1380, respectively, they were succeeded by two boy kings: ten-year-old Richard II of England and eleven-year-old Charles VI of France. Their youth and significant civil unrest—such as the English Peasants' Revolt in 1381—brought a sudden end to the hostilities. While the 1383-1385 Portuguese interregnum was considered a proxy war, it did not have a significant strategic effect, and by 1389, the kings had signed the Truce of Leulinghem, ending the Caroline phase of the war and ushering in 25 years of uneasy peace.

Perhaps some believed that the war might even be over. Yet unrest continued in both countries. In 1392, Charles VI suddenly and unexpectedly experienced a moment of psychosis that caused him to kill one of his own knights. He was dragged back to his castle in bonds for his own safety, and sadly for his people, this would not be the last of these episodes. He would continue to experience hallucinations, delusions, and strange behavior for the rest of his life. Without a ruler, France found itself unable to do much fighting on a grand scale.

England itself was in no position to invade, either. Richard II was deposed by Henry of Bolingbroke, soon crowned Henry IV, who was surrounded on all sides by rebellions from England and Wales. France supported the Welsh rebellion, but it was crushed in 1415 by Henry IV's son, a particularly ruthless young man crowned King Henry V in 1413.

With peace established in his own country, Henry V set his sights on expanding his rule. And he knew that France, with its mad king, was a sitting duck.

Chapter 2 – A Whispered Prophecy

Illustration I: The house where Joan of Arc was born

France, 1415. Harfleur had just fallen to the English. The port had put up a courageous resistance, resulting in a siege that lasted over a month, despite Henry V's significantly superior forces. But on September 22nd, the city fell at last, and Henry established a firm foothold on French soil where he could receive reinforcements.

All of France trembled in its boots. There were several strong French military leaders at the time, but King Charles VI's bouts of madness had only intensified and become more frequent as age continued to take a toll on his poor mental health. Without a single unifying leader, the French army was floundering in the face of Henry's mighty force. Henry attacked with single-minded determination while the French nobility squabbled arrogantly among themselves, and the commoners found themselves over-taxed and uninspired by their leadership. Many French nobles were starting to wonder if it wouldn't be better to just surrender to the English and allow themselves to be led by a king who was in full possession of his mental faculties, as well as being a gifted military leader.

But the commoners and many of the other nobles would have none of it. They were French, and they wanted to stay Frenchmen under a French king. And it was among these people that the prophecy had first started to circulate.

* * * *

As the English moved inexorably across the country, the prophecy flew from mouth to mouth. It was an old one, one that had long been recited, but the closer the English came, the faster the prophecy moved. A swift and whispered thing, it fled before the approaching horde.

No one is quite sure where the prophecy originally came from. Some attributed it to Saint Bede the Venerable, a monk and writer from the seventh century. Others believed it came from Euglide of Hungary, and still others thought it had been made by the mystical wizard from the time of King Arthur and his knights—Merlin. Wherever it came from and however old it was (no one knew for sure), it was suddenly remembered now. It was a desperate thing for a desperate time. And times grew ever more desperate as Henry swept across the country. City after city fell before him like wheat before the scythe, starting with the Battle of Agincourt, where the enormous French force could do nothing against the English. Caen fell. Then Rouen. By 1420, all of France was in great peril with the English swarming all over the countryside.

As fast as the English moved, the prophecy moved faster. It was on every set of lips and in every Frenchman's ear at that time. It was as simple as it was terrifying, as ominous as it was hopeful.

France will be lost by a woman, it said. *But it will be saved by a virgin from the borders of Lorraine.*

It was a strange prophecy for that time, considering that women were largely considered to have little role in politics and certainly no role in war. Even noblewomen were often used as a commodity at that time, being married off to improve alliances at their father's whim. Yet this prophecy seemed to say that two women would be able to change the fate of the whole of France, not once, but twice.

Perhaps at any other time, the prophecy would have been rejected. But not at this one. The people of France were desperate, and they clung to this prophecy with an iron grip.

* * * *

The French were well aware that the first part of their prophecy was about to come true—the part about France being lost by a woman. John the Fearless, Duke of Burgundy, had the potential to be one of France's key allies; but when jealous supporters of the Dauphin, also named Charles, assassinated him in Paris in 1419, the Burgundians switched sides to join forces with the English. Burgundy took Paris, and the capital was officially in the grasp of the enemy.

What the French didn't know was that the second part of the prophecy had already been set in motion. In 1412, even before Henry had landed in Harfleur, the Maid of France was born. Yet she was not born into the silken bedding of a noble house. Instead, she was brought forth in the peasant village of Domrémy in a modest but fairly typical peasant home—a crooked little building on a crooked little piece of pavement, bordered by the woods and the church. It was here, and not in some soaring palace or majestic castle, that the hero of France would spend her childhood. Domrémy itself was a small village of little consequence in the northeast of France near the border of Lorraine, then part of the Holy Roman Empire.

Jacques d'Arc was a farmer and a pillar of the community in the little village. He had some official duties in the village which helped to supplement his income on his small farm. His wife, Isabelle, was a housewife, as was typical of peasant women in this period, but she showed an unusual amount of piety—as evidenced by her nickname of Romée, a title that indicated she had undertaken a pilgrimage to Rome at some point before getting married, probably in her teens. She gave birth to her daughter on January 6th, 1412. The baby girl was named Jeanne d'Arc.

Like most peasant children, Jeanne did not go to school—education was a privilege reserved for the wealthy and the well-born. Instead, she spent her time helping her mother around the house, learning the duties of the medieval peasant woman: cooking, cleaning, tending to animals, and gardening. One place where she did go to learn, however, was church. Europe at the time was a profoundly Catholic continent, considering that the Roman Catholic Church was the only one in existence in that area, and so little Jeanne attended mass regularly, assisted by her deeply pious mother. Here, she learned all about the saints and, most importantly, about God.

All of the information that Jeanne received about God was given to her via a priest. Unlike modern Christians, Jeanne did not learn about Him on her own by reading the Bible. Although the Bible had been fully translated into French for the first time in 1377, this did not benefit the young Jeanne much: like most peasants, she could neither read nor write. But she could listen. And listen she did, with rapt attention beside her mother in mass, as she was told about this God who had created the world and set it all in motion. She was told about Jesus, the human incarnation of God, and His death on the cross to set all sinners free. And little Jeanne was immediately in love. Following her mother's dutiful example, she threw her heart and soul into the service of God, learning her prayers and following the commandments she'd been taught.

Perhaps, even as a small child, Jeanne knew how low-born she was. She was just a little peasant child and a girl to boot—arguably the least influential person in the length and breadth of France. But she had a courage and a faith that refused to be quenched.

* * * *

Jeanne was eight years old when France finally fell. Henry V, in his quest to obtain the throne, had made his way to Troyes, and it was here that the next treaty of the Hundred Years' War was signed. King Charles VI was still deep in his insanity, lost in a strange and paranoid world where anything could happen, and his son, the Dauphin, was an unpopular figure among the French, with rumors circulating that he had ordered the murder of the Duke of Burgundy and thus placed France in the position it now found itself. Queen Isabeau of France, the wife of Charles VI, decided that something would have to be done. She herself was no favorite of the French people. They had long believed that she had had an affair with Charles VI's brother, possibly resulting in the birth of the Dauphin. Now, however, she decided that she was done with being the queen of a beleaguered country. She agreed to sign a treaty with Henry that would declare the Dauphin illegitimate and give Henry the hand of her daughter, Princess Catherine, in marriage. The Treaty of Troyes was less of a treaty and more of a French surrender. By signing it, Henry was receiving not only a princess to wed but also succession to the French throne. Charles VI would reign until his death, but if Henry and Catherine had children, they would inherit the throne of France. France was one generation away from being under English control.

The first part of the prophecy had come true. Isabeau had signed away the Dauphin's birthright, losing France to the English. It had been lost by a woman. But it would be saved by a virgin.

Chapter 3 – The First Vision

In 1425, France had two kings.

King Charles VI, the poor mad king, had died on October 21st, 1422. Not long before, his archenemy King Henry V had also passed away. Immediately, the English hurried to crown King Henry V's tiny son: a mere baby who became King Henry VI. But the Dauphin Charles, who controlled just a few territories around Bourges, also laid claim to the throne despite the treaty that had declared him illegitimate. Charles had grown up believing that he would someday be king and to have this right snatched away so cruelly by a mere babe was more than he could bear. While he was not officially crowned yet, he determined that he was the rightful king and started to tighten his grip on the central provinces of France that he still controlled. An English child may have been the official king of France, but the war raged on. Led by the Earl of Salisbury, the English army was determined to pry the last of Charles's territories out of his desperate grip. They defeated a huge French force at the Battle of Verneuil in 1424, a fight that eerily echoed the Battle of Agincourt. City after city fell, and Charles was derisively known as the "King of Bourges" since that was about all that he had under his control.

France was all but lost. Yet innocent little Jeanne d'Arc was about to experience the first event that would eventually see her transformed into the heroine of France.

* * * *

It was in 1425 that Jeanne had her first taste of what the war really meant. A thirteen-year-old girl at that point, she was poised on the threshold of adulthood, yet most of her time was occupied with ordinary household chores and simple acts of everyday piety that would not appear to be anything other than mundane. The territory surrounding Domrémy had been captured by the English army, who had gone on to fight bigger battles; Jeanne herself had seen very little of the fighting. Her father's income was stable, and as far as Jeanne was aware, the village may as well have been experiencing a time of peace.

But it did not last long. Henry of Orly, a ruthless mercenary, had a castle nearby. In these last decades of the war, neither the English nor the French were really capable of paying their soldiers; instead, most soldiers turned to pillaging the surrounding countryside in order to gain some recompense for their services. Henry was the worst of these. Loyal to no one except himself, he took advantage of a country torn by war to live a careless existence as a freebooter. He allied himself with whoever would be most advantageous to him at the time and was mostly occupied with gaining loot for himself. And one day, he decided that his next booty would be coming from Domrémy. Accompanied by his wild band of mercenaries, he descended upon the little village, sowing terror in the streets. The panicking villagers hardly knew where to flee; they expected that he would burn the houses down but remaining outside meant they would be sliced down with a sword. There was a castle nearby where they could seek shelter, but Henry came too quickly. Jeanne's peaceful little village was suddenly filled with shouting and cackling hordes of careless and dirty men, their horses' hooves clanging on the street, their swords and armor flashing in the sun. Panicking people were running in all directions. But Henry wasn't after the peasants' lives. He was after their cattle. Gathering every last piece of livestock in the village, he headed back for his castle with the lot of them, leaving the peasants alive but stripped of their means of supporting themselves and their families.

The villagers appealed to the count of Vaudemont, who quickly defeated Henry and restored the cattle to their rightful owners. Real harm was avoided, but the damage was done to the frightened peasants' psyche. Even though Vaudemont served the English, the peasants made up their minds that the war was directly responsible for the tragedy they had so nearly suffered. A common consensus was reached among them that there would be no peace and quiet until the English were driven from France once and for all.

It's likely that the prophecy was mentioned again and again in the village at this time, and that many of the villagers had hung their hopes on a lady heroine riding in on a white stallion. As for Jeanne, perhaps she hoped for the same thing. Either way, with the cattle brought back, she returned to her everyday life of doing her chores.

One of these chores was tending her father's garden. It was a strip of ground between Jeanne's house and the church where she always attended mass, and as one of the older children in the house, Jeanne was expected to tend it well. One sweltering summer day, Jeanne was hard at work in the garden. The sun was high in the sky, and sweat dripped down her young brow as she bent over the rich earth. A flash of light by the church caught her eye. She paused, rubbing her eyes, which stung with sweat. Was it just reflecting sunlight which caused the sudden burst of radiance? Yet something inside her prompted her to look again, something strangely exciting that had her a little scared. She swallowed, looking to her left, and that was when she saw him. Blinding light filled the garden, a dazzling glow that she had never seen before. Wreathed in the beams of light, she saw an angel—a towering figure, gleaming in brazen armor, with spreading wings rising up from his shoulders. He was as terrifying as he was beautiful, and Jeanne would have fled if she'd felt that she could. Instead, rooted to the spot, she just gazed up at him as his wings were thrown wide, filling her world.

She didn't have to ask the angel who he was. He was so big, so bright, and so powerful that he could only have been Michael, the archangel. He stood above her in dazzling splendor, and she could only stare. Soon, two more figures appeared beside him, both beautiful young women, and Jeanne recognized them at once. The first was Saint Catherine of Alexandria, a courageous princess who had defied the Roman Emperor Maxentius when he began to persecute Christians; Maxentius had tried everything to make her renounce her faith, from threatening the death penalty to offering to marry her, but nothing had worked. Catherine had been beheaded as a mere teenager, dying a defiant virgin, a young woman who refused to allow her faith to be broken.

The other was Saint Margaret of Antioch. Like Catherine, Margaret was a teenage martyr, the daughter of a pagan priest who promptly disowned her when she became a Christian. A Roman governor attempted to marry her, but she, too, clung to her faith and virginity. She was tortured and killed at a young age.

While it is uncertain where Jeanne could have learned about these two young women, their appearance in her first vision was something eerily prophetic. She didn't know how similar a path she was bound to walk one day. She was just a thirteen-year-old girl looking up into the faces of saints and angels in mute awe. The saints were far from the tattered teens that had been killed for their faith; now, they wore splendid, golden crowns, decked with jewels, and their faces were radiant to look upon.

Terrified, Jeanne fell to her knees. The saints hurried to reassure her that they had been sent to her by God. They went on to tell her that God had placed a high calling on her life, given her a tremendous duty to fulfill, not now but soon. He wanted her to drive the English out of France. And He wanted her to get the Dauphin to Reims and crown him king.

Then the saints were gone. Jeanne realized that she was sitting motionless in the garden, tears pouring down her cheeks. She wept not with fear but with a kind of trembling awe at the saints she had just beheld and the weight of their words to her. She didn't know why they would come to her, to little Jeanne d'Arc, an illiterate peasant girl living on the edge of France, but one thing she did know: what God told her to do, she would do.

Chapter 4 – The Doubt of Baudricourt

Over the next three years, the saints continued to visit Jeanne as she grew up in her father's house. Almost every day, the divine light would fill Jeanne's vision, and she would hear their voices telling her again that she needed to crown the Dauphin, that she was going to lead the army that would finally give France victory over the English. Every day, she grew more and more used to the saints and even began to converse with them. Yet for three years, Jeanne remained in her father's house, and she told no one.

As she was now reaching her mid-teens, Jeanne would have been considered a marriageable age. Her father, Jacques, likely was already looking around for a suitor that would be able to give Jeanne a stable and comfortable existence. But Jacques himself was about to have a dream—one that would terrify any father's heart.

One night, before Jeanne had even started to consider leaving the house, Jacques had a dream. In it, he saw his gentle and lovely daughter mounted on a horse and leaving their village with a group of rough-looking men—he knew they must be soldiers. Jacques awoke with a sweaty brow and a pounding heart. It couldn't be. Surely not his Jeanne, his sweet, pious little girl. At that moment, the prophecy was the furthest thing from Jacques's mind; Jeanne was just a peasant girl, no savior of the nation. Instead, Jacques assumed that what he'd seen in his dream was Jeanne joining the army as a prostitute. The dream was disturbing enough that he told his sons that if it ever came true, they were to drown Jeanne rather than let her sell herself in that way.

Jacques's dream would soon come true but not in the way that he thought. Jeanne was going to leave. And she was going to leave on a quest of purity and power.

* * * *

Across France, things had never looked bleaker for the disinherited Dauphin. In August 1428, the English—led primarily by the Earl of Salisbury—had landed at Calais. Joined by allies from Bedford, the English army had been swollen to a force ten thousand strong. Their intentions were clear: they were going to drive out any who dared to oppose the baby King Henry VI, claim back the territories that Charles was still clinging to, and make France an English colony once and for all.

Within a few weeks, multiple French cities had fallen before the English horde. Chartres, Janville, Meung, Beaugency, Jargeau—they didn't stand a chance. One by one they all fell at the earl's feet, and he set his sights on Orléans.

He could never have guessed how the siege of that city would end.

* * * *

In May 1428, as the French countryside was blossoming into the vivid colors of spring, Jeanne's voices started to speak to her with increasing intensity. They had long been urging her that it was time to go and meet the Dauphin, and Jeanne, seeing how ludicrous the very idea was, had been hesitating. But the voices insisted, saying that it was God's will that she needed to go and save their nation. They urged her that the Lord had chosen her for a reason. If some duke or noble was to ride forth and reclaim France, then it would be evident that the fight had been won by a man, but if a mere peasant girl like Jeanne did it, glory could only be to God. It made sense, and Jeanne finally realized that she could resist the voices no more.

She knew that the nearest garrison that remained loyal to Charles was at Vaucouleurs, a city about twelve miles from Domrémy. Once she acquiesced to her mission, her voices told her that she was to go there and appeal to Robert de Baudricourt—the captain of the garrison—for an audience with the Dauphin and safe passage to Chinon, where he was stationed at the time. Jeanne's first cousin, Durand Laxart, stayed only a few miles outside of Vaucouleurs. Telling her parents that she wanted to go and visit him, Jeanne succeeded in persuading Durand to come and pick her up at Domrémy for a visit with him and his wife, her cousin Jeanne Laxart.

During the drive, Durand could sense that there was something different about young Jeanne. Something had changed in the bright blue of her eyes; there was a presence about her, a glow that he couldn't quite place. He didn't ask, however, concentrating on the road instead as his horse took them briskly toward home. At last—it is uncertain whether this happened during the drive or in Durand's home—Jeanne opened up, talking about her visions for the first time. Gathering her courage, she told Durand that she needed to go "into France" (referring to central France, the area still governed by the Dauphin).

"Why?" her first cousin inquired, knowing that central France was a war zone.

"I need to crown the Dauphin at Reims," Jeanne answered calmly.

Durand stared at her, wondering if she knew how ridiculous her words were. But those blue eyes remained as serene as still pools of deep water as she studied him, her voice steady and sure. "Has it not been said," she added, "that France would be ruined by a woman and later restored by a virgin?"

Durand didn't know what to say. He knew as well as any Frenchman that Isabeau had signed away her own country, and he had heard the prophecy over and over again. Yet he had never imagined that this virgin savior could come from a place like Domrémy, that it could be a peasant girl, that it could be *this* little peasant girl, his own cousin Jeanne d'Arc.

She went on to tell him that she had to get to Vaucouleurs and to Robert de Baudricourt. And perhaps it was the fire in her eyes or perhaps it was the desperation in Durand's own heart, but he decided that he believed her. He vowed that he would take her to Vaucouleurs and get her that audience with the captain, no matter how crazy it would make him look.

* * * *

Robert de Baudricourt was captain of the small garrison at Vaucouleurs. Itself a small town, Vaucouleurs was so familiar to the twenty-eight-year-old captain that he knew almost every face in it. He certainly recognized Durand Laxart, but as for the girl following him, she was a stranger to him. There was something ethereal about her as she approached. She wore a torn, tattered red dress, a faded thing that had been mended often; her body was slender, her features pinched, but those eyes. They were an almost indefinable shade of blue, and the light inside them made Robert stare for a few moments as Durand walked past. When the girl's eyes rested on him, she stopped, her face lighting up in recognition even though Robert knew he had never seen her before. She grabbed Durand's arm and pointed, and they made their way up to Robert.

Durand introduced Jeanne as his cousin who was staying with him for a while. Bemused, Robert asked her what she wanted, expecting her to have some foolish request that he could easily push aside. Instead, the girl spoke with a clarity and a strength that he had not been expecting.

"I have come to you on the part of my Lord," she told him, "in order that you may send word to the Dauphin, to hold fast, and to not cease war against his enemies."

Robert blinked. He was only a minor noble, one who had likely never actually exchanged a single word with the Dauphin, let alone told him what to do. Before he could demand who this Jeanne thought she was—or who she thought *he* was to have that kind of authority—she went on. "Before mid-Lent, the Lord will give him help," she told him. "In truth, the kingdom belongs not to the Dauphin but to my Lord."

Angered, Robert glared at her. He was one of the last Dauphin loyalists left in one of the last cities in the area that would still dare to voice its alliance to him instead of submitting to the Anglo-Burgundians. He was about to rebuke her for assuming that anyone other than the Dauphin Charles could be made king when she interrupted. "But my Lord wills that the Dauphin be made king and have the kingdom in [his] command. Notwithstanding his enemies, the Dauphin will be made king." She raised her chin, her eyes filled with something that was nothing like pride but as sure as steel. "And it is I that will conduct him to the coronation."

It was all that Robert could do not to burst out laughing. This raggedy peasant girl seemed to truly believe that she was going to crown the Dauphin, despite the fact that she could never even behold his face with her low-born status. "And who is this Lord of yours?" he demanded.

"God," Jeanne replied simply.

Robert shook his head with a derisive snort. Turning to Durand, he said, "Take this girl back to her father and box her ears." Then he dismissed them with a flick of his hand.

* * * *

Jeanne was immediately dismayed by Robert's reaction to her request. Subdued, she asked Durand to take her back home to her father. Heartbroken for his cousin's unhappiness, awed by her ability to somehow recognize Robert even though she had never seen him before, and upset at Robert's reaction, Durand dutifully drove her back home to Domrémy.

That could have been the last that anyone ever heard of Jeanne d'Arc. But things were about to take a turn for the worse in the war and in everyday life in Domrémy—a turn that would inspire Jeanne to go back to Vaucouleurs. And this time, she would have help.

Chapter 5 – A Prediction of Defeat

Illustration II: 15th-century Orléans

After conquering Meung on September 8th, 1428, the Earl of Salisbury knew that he was ready to press home his advantage. There was one last major obstacle standing between him and central France which was controlled by the Dauphin. That obstacle was the Loire River, and it was guarded by the city of Orléans. Also at the time the capital of the duchy of Orléans, it was of political as well as strategic importance. Taking it down would be breaking apart the last wall that stood between the English and the heart of France, and if Orléans fell, the Dauphin's claim to the throne would be all but lost.

The city itself was built on the northern shore of the Loire, and the only way to access it was via a bridge guarded by a gatehouse named Les Tourelles. It was at the Tourelles that the Earl of Salisbury mounted his first attack on October 12th, 1428. The Siege of Orléans had begun. And if that city fell, France would be doomed.

* * * *

Just before the siege began, Jeanne had started feeling the effects of the war once again.

A few weeks after her return to Domrémy, the English and Burgundians decided that Vaucouleurs, in its puny defiance, was a thorn in the side that they would no longer tolerate. It may have been a small town, but it was a loyal one to the Dauphin, and it was time to beat its inhabitants—and those of the surrounding villagers—into submission. The first warning that Jeanne had was the deafening ringing of the church bell next door to her home. Its sound, normally so melodious, was now a cacophonous clang as the bell-ringer pulled desperately at the rope, pealing a loud warning through the streets of Domrémy. The d'Arc family had no choice but to flee. Taking Jeanne with them, they had to drive their cattle across open territory to the fortified Neufchâteau, where they were forced to seek shelter in an inn.

When the army was gone, Jeanne and her family returned to a ruined Domrémy. Fields and houses were damaged by fire and wanton destruction. The English had not cared how peace-loving the peasants of Domrémy were; they belonged to the French, and thus they were enemies, no matter how uninvolved they really were in the war. Worst of all, they had burned the church. The sight broke Jeanne's heart. Her saints had never stopped urging her to get back to Vaucouleurs and find her way to the Dauphin, and as soon as the fighting in the immediate vicinity was over, that was exactly what she did.

* * * *

There was something final about Jeanne's second departure from the village where she'd grown up. Her heart was torn to leave her parents and still more torn by the untruth she told them—that she was leaving in order to act as a nurse and helper for Jeanne Laxart, who was expecting a baby. In truth, part of Jeanne's soul knew that she would never see idyllic Domrémy again. She watched it fade into the distance, its quaint little church, its snowbound fields, its beautiful wood, the garden where she'd first heard the voices, and knew in her heart of hearts that she would never go back.

It was January 1429. The Siege of Orléans had been raging for three months, and there was still no end in sight. French reinforcements had been able to squeeze through the English lines here and there, enabling the city to hang on far longer than expected. The death of the Earl of Salisbury had been a setback for England, but he was replaced by the Earl of Suffolk, and the siege continued undeterred. For months, small skirmishes had been sparking all over the city, but it was generally at something of a stalemate, with the French stubbornly holding on within the walls and the English firmly dug in outside them. All of central France hung in nervous limbo, with the might of the English encamped only about seventy-five miles from the administrative capital of Bourges.

Jeanne didn't know much about the details. Rumors among the peasants would likely have told her that a siege had been laid to Orléans, but apart from this, no one would have given an ignorant little peasant much information. She knew that the voices were urging her more and more intensely to go back to Vaucouleurs, and that was enough for her.

Arriving at Vaucouleurs, Jeanne lodged with the Leroyer family, where she worked as a servant to Henri and Catherine Leroyer. It was here that she first really caught the eye of Jean de Metz. One of Robert's squires, Jean had been present during her first meeting with Robert, and something about the girl's glittering presence inspired him. When he spotted her heading toward the garrison once more, he knew he had to speak to her.

Approaching her, he hoped she would recognize him from her first meeting with Baudricourt. "What are you doing here, my friend?" he asked. Suddenly nervous faced with her innocent blue eyes, Jean fumbled, trying to make some small talk. The war was the first thing that came to mind; it had been going on for so many decades that talking about the war was like talking about the weather. "Must the King be driven from the kingdom?" he said conversationally. "And are we to be English?"

Jeanne studied him for a few seconds. Her eyes were completely serene as she spoke. "I am come here to this royal town to speak to Robert de Baudricourt," she said.

Jean was not surprised. He had known, despite the defeat in her eyes the last time she met with his master, that Jeanne would not give up so easily. She went on to explain again that she needed Robert to take her to the king but that he hadn't taken her or her words seriously. "Nevertheless, before the middle of Lent, I must be with the King," she said. "There is no succor to be expected save from me."

The quiet confidence in her words took Jean by surprise. He studied her, wondering how this work-worn peasant girl could possibly have come to this conclusion. She added that she would rather have stayed home, spinning wool with her mother, but that she had to go to the King "because my Lord wills that I should do it."

The way she said the Lord's name rang with authority. Looking at her bearing, at the complete lack of arrogance in the way she held herself, and in the utter conviction in her tone, Jean knew she was speaking the truth. Somehow, God had chosen this girl, this piece of nothing in the face of a haughty society, to save the nation of France from the marauding English. He reached out, taking her small hand in his. It was rough and hard from manual labor. "With God's guidance, I promise, I will conduct you to the King," he said.

* * * *

Between Jean and another knight and fellow supporter of Jeanne, Bertrand de Poulengy, they succeeded in securing another audience with Robert for her. Dubious though Robert was, he couldn't seem to forget the light in the eyes of the young girl with her crazy claims that had visited him last spring. Now she was back, here in the crispness of February 12th, 1429, and Robert was getting desperate. Vaucouleurs had suffered during the war, Orléans was besieged, and France was all but lost. It couldn't hurt to hear out this little lunatic.

Upon meeting with Robert, Jeanne told him, again, what she wanted from him: to be taken safely through enemy territory to meet with the Dauphin. Then she added that the Dauphin's forces were about to suffer a terrible defeat.

As Jeanne spoke to Robert, hundreds of miles away on a great flat plain near Rouvray, there was the crack of gunpowder and the whine of cannonballs launching through the air. 1,600 Englishmen dived for cover as cannonballs punched into their wagon train. It had been drawn into a makeshift defensive formation, with sharpened spikes plunged into the earth around the wagon train in a bid to hold off the French, but the English were well aware that there were twice as many men in the attacking Franco-Scottish army as in this baggage train. Wagons splintered, supplies spilling out onto the ground: barrels of herring, stacks of artillery. Hope leaped in the hearts of the French army. If they could stop this baggage train from reaching Orléans, the siege might just be over.

"What?" Robert stared at the girl. "What do you mean?"

"The Dauphin's arms have this day suffered a great reverse near Orléans," Jeanne repeated.

It was madness, Robert thought. Yet the calm conviction in her eyes chilled him to the core.

There was a shout of dismay from the French. The Scottish part of their army was charging, overexcited by the damage the cannons had inflicted on the English. The French had to cease fire, and the

English rose, firing with crossbows and longbows from behind their wagons. The Scottish ranks crumbled, men dying in all directions. The French were forced to lead a cavalry charge that they knew would be ineffective against the English archers. They were right. In minutes, the English led a counterattack, and the French and Scottish were ignominiously routed.

"Get out," Robert ordered Jeanne. "Go."

* * * *

A few days later, the news reached Vaucouleurs. The Franco-Scottish army had tried to stop a baggage train from reaching Orléans and horribly failed, losing about six hundred men, while the English lost only four. It was a humiliating defeat, since known as the Battle of the Herrings.

When Robert heard the news, and heard that the fight had taken place on the same day as his meeting with Jeanne, he knew that her prediction had been true. And if that was true, maybe it was also true that she was the savior of France.

He called her to his garrison and told her that he would send her to Chinon with Jean and Bertrand. His words were those of a desperate man, still doubting but unable to find any other shred of hope to cling to. "Go," he told her. "And let come what may."

Chapter 6 – An Audience with the King

The road to Chinon was fraught with danger. Charles's court was about three hundred miles away from Vaucouleurs, a distance that would take at least a week of hard riding, but that was the least of Jean's and Bertrand's worries as they considered how best to escort their young and innocent charge to the court of the Dauphin. The truth was that Vaucouleurs and its surrounding villages were some of the most isolated territories remaining under French control. To reach Chinon, they would have to cross a vast expanse of enemy territory, effectively trespassing on the lands of the infant English king. Somehow they had to get to Chinon without attracting enemy attention, which would have been hard enough for a group of men, let alone only a few knights guarding a vulnerable young woman who had no experience of war and—it seemed—little comprehension of danger.

Together with the people of Vaucouleurs, who had noticed Jeanne's repeated visits to Robert and learned via rumors of her quest, Jean and Bertrand decided that the safest way to get Jeanne to Chinon would be to disguise her as a man. Jeanne willingly agreed with the idea, despite the fact that cross-dressing was widely considered to be a heinous crime in that era; however, Jeanne and everyone she spoke to thought of it as a normal and necessary precaution against attack from those who might want to carry her off and have their way with her. Luckily for Jeanne, she had become something of a sensation in Vaucouleurs. Long known as a virtuous and kind girl—albeit a little odd—she had suddenly become the hope of the hopeless. The mere fact that Robert was willing to send her to Chinon at all gave her credibility in the eyes of the people. They believed that she was going to save them and the rest of their nation from the English, and they would do anything for her. Making her some suitable clothing for the journey was the least they could do.

While this was being undertaken, Jean headed off and bought a horse. The people of Vaucouleurs presented Jeanne with a sword as well as the clothing, and she was well disguised as a fellow knight when she set off with her small retinue: Jean, Bertrand, and two other men-at-arms. Bertrand paid for the journey. They left Vaucouleurs on February 23rd, 1429, beginning their perilous journey through an area that was controlled by the Burgundians at the time.

For ten days, Jeanne and her companions rode by night and slept by day, using little lanes and forgotten roadways to avoid detection by their enemies. It must have been a strange and new experience for the innocent young Jeanne, riding a strong and lively horse in between a group of rough soldiers. It's unlikely that she had ever ridden much considering her family's lowly status; she would also have never worn anything like the hosen (tight pants) that she found herself in now. Everything would have been new and uncomfortable for her, and she was traveling more in a day than she ever had in her entire life. Yet her two guardians would later testify that she remained her sweet, gentle self. Not a single curse passed her lips, nor did she conduct herself with anything other than calm confidence. Even the seasoned warriors were fearing for their lives as they traversed the dangerous landscape, but Jeanne showed no fear. She told them that it was God's will for them to get to Chinon, and get to Chinon they would.

Jeanne also owed much of her safety to the two knights who so fervently believed in her. They never left her side. At night, she slept safely between the two of them, who would rather have cut off their own heads than lay a finger on the young maiden lying so close.

The only thing that really troubled Jeanne during the journey was that she wanted to go to Mass. As the churches were occupied by the English and there was some risk that the French knights would have been identified, this was impossible.

Finally, on March 6th, 1429, they reached Chinon at last, utterly unharmed. The perilous journey was over. But now, Jeanne had to do more than convince a lowly captain of the guard to grant her passage to Chinon. She had to get herself an audience with the Dauphin himself.

* * * *

The Dauphin Charles was a desperate man. Despite being only twenty-six years old, he had had everything taken from him. Having grown up in a household with a mentally ill father whose rampages were, by turns, humiliating and dangerous, Charles's great hope had been the knowledge that he would someday be king—a better king by far than his mad predecessor.

Then came the terrible blow dealt to him by his own mother, Isabeau. Supporting the rumors that said that Charles was an illegitimate product of an affair between Isabeau and his uncle Louis, she signed away her own son's birthright to his greatest enemy. The bitterness of it was terrible, and Charles was aware that despite the fact that he saw himself as the rightful king of France, he had little hope of ever claiming his throne. The English were at his very threshold. It would not be long before his army fell and his country belonged to some English baby.

In fact, Charles had all but given up hope. He hung around in Chinon now, watching the progress of the war with a numbed sense of inevitable defeat. He was doomed. He always had been.

He was in this state when one of his courtiers came to inform him that a strange young woman had just arrived in Chinon; a mere peasant girl, dressed as a young man, bearing a sword and astride a horse. Her name, the courtier told him, was Jeanne d'Arc. She said that she was going to save the nation of France. She said that God had sent her.

At first, Charles wanted to laugh. But somehow, the idea sparked a flicker of interest in him. He had nothing left to lose—everything had been stripped from him. Hearing this girl out was a desperate measure, but he was a desperate man. She would have to prove, however, that she really did have divine help. He decided that he was going to dress as an ordinary courtier and then have Jeanne brought into a room full of similarly dressed men. If she could identify him, he would grant her a personal audience. This was an age before photographs; in wartime France, some peasant girl from hundreds of miles away would have no idea what the Dauphin looked like.

All was done as Charles ordered. The courtiers were all gathered together, slightly unnerved by seeing their Dauphin dressed like them, and another courtier was told to pretend to be the king once Jeanne had made her selection. Faintly bored and apathetic, Charles waited for the appearance of this girl who said that the saints were talking to her.

The doors opened, and Jeanne was shown in. Charles was struck by her at once. Her hair had been roughly cut short, but there was no hiding her willowy figure, her glittering eyes. There was something about her that commanded his attention, and all eyes were on the girl as she walked into the room, her eyes wandering along the lines of courtiers. She seemed focused inward somehow, as if listening to something that only she could hear. A faint smile played on her lips as she gazed from face to face. When her eyes lit on Charles, the incredible happened. Her eyes widened in recognition, and she rushed up to him, her eyes locked on his for a breathtaking moment. Then she fell to her knees, throwing her arms around his legs. Their grip held the strength of a girl who had spent her life working. "God give you a happy life, sweet King!" she cried out.

Charles was stunned, but he managed to keep it together. Pulling away from her, he chided her, telling her that he was no king. Shaken though he was, the courtier that had been designated to play the role of the Dauphin stepped forward, saying that he was the king of France. But Jeanne would not be fooled. She continued to stay close to Charles, repeating over and over that he was the king, that her voices had told her so.

Awestruck, Charles gladly did what he had agreed to do: he granted her a private audience. Maybe, just maybe, the God that he felt had abandoned him for his entire life had finally decided to have mercy—and if He chose to do so through this random little peasant girl, Charles, royal though he was, was in no position to argue.

Chapter 7 – The Road to Orléans

Illustration III: Jeanne with her armor and famous banner

The details of Charles's private audience with Jeanne have never really been known to anyone, except for Charles and Jeanne themselves. Some sources say that Jeanne told him about a private prayer, something intensely personal and a secret that he had never shared with anyone. According to some, this prayer involved Charles's claim to the throne, but in it, the defeated Dauphin did not petition the Lord to bring him to the throne. Instead, in paralyzing insecurity, Charles begged God to punish himself alone instead of all the people if he truly was an illegitimate heir. The question had been plaguing him for years. He had no idea if he really was the product of a lawful union between the king and queen; perhaps he was illegitimate after all, the result of a cheating queen and a deceitful brother. Yet he couldn't tell his people that even he doubted his own legitimacy. He could only tell this to God, and he did so in a heartfelt prayer, pouring out his fear and agony in private.

Except Jeanne knew. She told him all about it, and she assured him that he was the rightful king, that it was the blood of Charles the Mad in his veins after all, and that it was God's will for him to ascend to the throne.

This is all speculation, however. Jeanne herself was tight-lipped for the rest of her life about this meeting, refusing to reveal any confidential details. Yet one thing is absolutely for certain: Jeanne made an impression on the Dauphin that left little doubt in his mind that God really had sent her, and that she really had the potential to save France from its overwhelming enemy.

The Dauphin's advisers were not as easily convinced, despite the fact that after his meeting with Jeanne, Charles was a changed man. Whatever she had said to him, it left him radiant, glowing with a new courage and conviction that they knew promised to be beneficial to the people who were desperate for a brave and motivated leader. However, they knew that caution had to be exercised. If Jeanne turned out to be some witch or heretic, the entire question of Charles's legitimacy would once again be raised even if he was able to get his throne back.

On their advice, Charles decided that Jeanne would be sent to Poitiers—the last theological establishment still within the Dauphin's control—to be thoroughly examined. She arrived there on March

11th, 1429, only a few days after her audience with the Dauphin, and stayed with Charles's advocate in Parliament. Some of the leading theologians left in France were there to conduct the examination, including doctors in theology, abbots, bishops, and several councilors who were educated in law. If there was a blemish on Jeanne's character or a reason to doubt her faith, these people would find it.

And so, a simple, illiterate farm girl from Domrémy found herself the subject of fierce scrutiny by some of the most educated men in the country. As much as France was desperate for a hero—or heroine, as it seemed—these men were determined to thoroughly prove if she was telling the truth. They knew that she was uneducated, that she was, to all accounts, a mere nobody, and they knew that the implications of sending her to the front and then seeing her fail would be enormous. She could be the last piece of hope the French had, and if that hope turned out to be false, morale would plummet and the war would be lost already. The theologians decided to show her no mercy and take no prisoners, simple though she might have seemed to be.

It was quickly evident that, as sweet as Jeanne was, she was no fool, nor was she even remotely intimidated by the important men who were questioning her. She firmly believed that the God of Heaven was on her side, and compared to Him, the theologians were nothing. They quickly started to question her about the voices she heard, trying to establish if they were saints or simply figments of an insane mind. One of the first questions, asked by Brother Seguin de Seguin, a professor of theology, was about the dialect that the saints spoke to her. "A better one than you," Jeanne answered with fierce calm.

Taken aback and yet somehow charmed by her fearlessness, Seguin looked her directly in the eyes and asked the simplest question of all. "Do you believe in God?"

Those bright blue eyes seemed to be staring directly into his soul. "In truth," she responded, "more than yourself!"

Seguin was surprised by her answer but impressed by the way in which she said it. There was no pride in her, only a sturdy assurance that he couldn't seem to find his way around. He told her that as much as she may believe in God, she couldn't prove that He had really sent her unless she gave the court some kind of a sign—a miracle from above to prove that what she told them was true. Throughout the interrogation, Jeanne had been asserting that she was going to break the siege at Orléans and crown Charles at Reims. When Seguin asked for a sign, Jeanne folded her arms in defiance. "I am not come to Poitiers to show signs," she retorted. "Send me to Orléans, where I shall show you the signs by which I am sent."

For the next three weeks, Jeanne was not only questioned in the chapel at Poitiers, but she was also followed and watched in secret, as it was determined that her private life had to be impeccable as well for her to be deemed worthy of the hope that the people were so eager to place upon her shoulders. Yet both in the interrogation and in their surveillance of her daily activities, the theologians could find no fault in her. In April 1429, they sent word to the Dauphin. The fact that Jeanne was a fervent Christian, upstanding in every moral way and as devoted in her faith as she was courageous, was indisputable; but whether or not she really was going to be able to lift the siege as she promised, they couldn't say, although they considered it likely. Their suggestion was to send her to Orléans, and if she perished, then she perished. If she won the battle, then so much the better. The Dauphin was to send her there as a test, as she had requested.

* * * *

During Jeanne's examination in Poitiers, a relief expedition was being planned to go to Orléans in a bid to free the beleaguered city from the English. Once her examination was over, Jeanne saw the expedition as an ideal opportunity to make her way to Orléans. Considering that she'd passed the test with flying colors, Charles had little choice other than to allow her to go—although it is likely that he was not reluctant to send her there, believing, as many of the

French people did, that Jeanne was the heroine they'd been waiting for. The Maiden that all the prophecies had foretold.

It didn't take long for her newfound credibility to reach the ears of the rich and noble, either. They pulled together to donate everything that Jeanne needed, pouring their money into this new hope. A suit of armor was created specifically for her in order to fit her feminine curves; she was given a sword and a shining white stallion, and finally, a banner. This banner was a simple thing—a depiction of Jesus, holding the world in His hands, flanked by two angels on a white background—but it would soon become the most powerful weapon in the Hundred Years' War. For while it would shed no blood, the whole army of France would rally behind it.

Chapter 8 – Arrival at Orléans

The French soldiers knew that they were on the brink of defeat.

They had been trapped inside Orléans for almost six months, watching the English fortifications grow, aware that with every passing day their enemies were mining underneath the French defenses, pushing their fortifications slowly nearer and nearer to the city walls. Worse, for five long months, only a handful of supply convoys had been able to make it through to the city. The English might not have been able to fully surround Orléans, but they had enough forces that any convoy approaching it had to take a long roundabout route through enemy territory, resulting in many convoys being discovered and captured. The English knew that they didn't have enough men to win the battle by direct assault. So, they decided to starve it to death instead.

It was working. Five months of hunger were taking their toll on the soldiers' morale. The fact that the English convoys were making it through—even when opposed by a significantly larger army, as demonstrated in the Battle of Herrings—didn't help. Soldiers and citizens of the city alike had to watch as the English feasted happily in their trenches, while inside Orléans, people went to bed on empty stomachs.

Rumors were circulating around the city that Orléans was on the brink of surrender, further causing morale to plummet. In fact, Orléans had already made an offer of surrender to Duke Philip III of Burgundy, and it was an offer that he found very attractive. Not only would control over the city allow his English allies to continue their campaign into central France, but half of its taxes would go to Burgundy as well, and Burgundy would be allowed to appoint its governors. In early April, Philip hurried to Paris, asking the English regent—the Duke of Bedford—to lift the siege so that Philip could accept the terms of surrender.

The Duke of Bedford refused absolutely. He was delighted by the news of this proposal, knowing that it meant Orléans had been brought to its knees. All that was left now was to deliver the *coup de grace*. Surely, in only a few weeks, Orléans would fall. According to medieval law and tradition, the citizens of a city that had resisted a siege (and no city had resisted more strenuously than Orléans) could be killed by an invading army once they had entered. It would be a bloodbath, and whatever citizens of Orléans were left would be slaves of the English. Bedford's control over Orléans would be absolute, and he was confident that it was only a matter of time before the city fell once and for all.

The situation was so dire for France that the Dauphin Charles's advisers were telling him that the French throne was a lost cause. Abdicating and fleeing to Scotland was the only option that would allow him to lead a peaceful and relatively free life; death or capture awaited should he continue to pursue the crown that was his birthright. But Charles refused to listen. A new hope had been awakened in him. And that hope was on its way to Orléans, dressed in a special suit of armor, riding a white stallion, and holding a white banner.

* * * *

Whispers of this mysterious girl had been flying through Orléans for almost two months. She was a virgin, they all said, a young girl from the borders of Lorraine who had been to see the Dauphin, and made such an impression on him that she was at that very moment on her way to Orléans with a much-needed relief expedition. And did not the prophecy say that such a girl would be the one to save the nation of France? It was the only piece of hope that the French soldiers had left, and they clung to it fiercely.

When news came that the relief expedition had almost reached Orléans and that one of its key commanders, Jean de Dunois, had headed out to meet it, excitement filled the hearts of the waiting soldiers. Men-at-arms and civilians alike started to gather in the streets, a murmur of excitement running through the crowd. Could it be true? Was she really here? Had God really sent her, as she'd told the Dauphin? They said that they had tested her at Poitiers and she had passed the test. Were they about to be saved?

More whispers filled the streets. The boats had gone out across the Loire to meet the relief expedition a few miles east of Orléans. When this mysterious maiden had gotten into the boat, the wind had magically changed, and they were sailing swiftly and under cover of darkness back to the city. It was a miracle, they were saying, though many doubted that the story was true. Yet even they had to hope that she had help from above.

Then they saw her. They saw the banner first, waving above the heads of the crowd, a shining white flag that waved in the breeze. Then she emerged, riding down the streets on a white charger that champed and snorted and pulled at the bit, yet this small and wispy young girl seemed to control him with ease. She wore a suit of plate armor and a wide-eyed smile, and when they looked into her bright blue eyes, they saw nothing but an unshakable confidence. It was something to believe in, and it threw the whole city of Orléans into rejoicing. They were cheering, dancing in the streets, praying out loud, praising God, chanting her name: *Jeanne d'Arc. Jeanne d'Arc.*

* * * *

Jeanne had not been idle during her journey to Orléans. Meeting her small army at Blois, she had proceeded to dictate a letter to the English, giving them a chance to flee from France before she and her army attacked. Her statements were as forceful as they were simple, asserting that God wanted the Dauphin Charles to be on the throne of France and that the English were to be gone—"Or I will make you go," she concluded. She signed her letter, simply, *La Pucelle*—The Maiden.

Of course, the English jeered at Jeanne's letters. Who was this simpleton, this mere peasant girl, to tell them to go, let alone somehow "make" them leave? They continued to insult and deprecate Jeanne when she was in Orléans, and she continued to send messengers to them demanding their retreat. The English were having none of it. They knew Orléans was on the edge of defeat, and they believed that their faith in this mad young girl was just another sign of their impending downfall. They called her a witch and a lunatic. It was on their lips that her name would first be spoken in English, a name that has gone down in history: Joan of Arc.

Joan didn't let any amount of English stubbornness deter her. When the English refused to back down, she ordered a charge against them. Jean de Dunois immediately put a stop to this, protesting that the garrison was too small to launch an offensive on the English—he would have to ride to Blois for still more reinforcements before this would be possible. On May 1st, he left the city, sneaking out to Blois. With his stern presence gone, Joan was free to do more or less whatever she wanted. She rode out of the city and inspected the English fortifications to the bemusement of the English warriors. They shouted various slurs at her from their fortifications but didn't attack her. After all, what did she know of battles? What damage could she possibly do? What threat could she possibly be?

Chapter 9 – Flying the White Banner

Illustration IV: Joan and her banner at the Siege of Orléans

Among the French army, Joan was rapidly gaining popularity. Now that more soldiers had actually set eyes on her, she was being called the Maid of France, the virgin savior who had been in the prophecies for so many years. The response was tremendous. French morale, which had been plundered by almost a century of war, suddenly began to climb. Deserters returned to the army, and suddenly, every brave young nobleman in France wanted to join up and strike a blow for the Dauphin because word had it that there was a saint at the front, that God was on their side. When Joan rode through the streets, she had to have an escort of knights with her or the exuberant crowd would snatch her right from her saddle in their excitement. They lined the streets everywhere she went, gazing at her in awe.

On May 4th, Dunois returned, bringing with him the suddenly swollen ranks of the bulk of the French army. He was surprised to see the sheer number of men that had either returned or joined thanks to the presence of Joan at Orléans. Joan rode out to meet the approaching army with a small group of men in case of attack, but despite the fact that the English were within sight, the army made it safely to Orléans. Joan and Dunois had dinner together that evening, and Dunois promised that he would send Joan's page boy to her with news if any combat took place.

However, it appears that Joan's page failed in his duties. That very night, Dunois and a group of 1,500 men launched an assault on an English bastille named St. Loup, and Joan was fast asleep when this took place. Suddenly, she woke and rushed to shake her attendant awake. Joan's words and thoughts were still vague and sluggish with sleep, but her message was urgent: her voices had told her that she had to go to battle. Rushing to scold her page for his misbehavior, Joan ordered him to fetch her horse while other attendants helped her into her armor. In a flurry of activity, Joan jumped onto her white stallion, seized her banner, and then set spurs to her horse, sending him galloping madly out of the city.

Followed by some of her companions, Joan rode toward St. Loup, and it was here that she witnessed what real battle was for the first time. For a gentle peasant girl, it would have been a horrible shock. Even though she had had to flee from the English before, never had she seen death and destruction on such a terrifying scale. Tears ran down her cheeks as she beheld the wounded being carried back to Orléans; worse still were the torn and gutted bodies of the soldiers who had lost their lives in the fight. They were scattered carelessly across the battlefield, their blood soaking into the earth, flies buzzing around their motionless limbs and walking across their glazed and staring eyes. Skin was torn aside, splintered bone brutally exposed, and innards were ripped and spilling from bloated bodies. This was battle, and it was real, with real blood on the dirt, the real stench of death in the air, and real people losing their lives.

As real as the fight was, Joan's faith was more real still. Ashen-faced and crying, Joan did not allow the horrific sight to stop her. She spurred her horse on and rode for St. Loup. Despite the fact that the French outnumbered the English garrison there more than three to one, they were struggling, facing yet another disheartening defeat until they heard a pure young voice cry out from the direction of Orléans. It was Joan. When the French saw her banner snapping above her head, its whiteness stark against the blue sky, they rallied. Petrified of the "witch," the English faltered. The French surged forward, pushing the English back to the bell tower of the fort, and within a few hours, the English had fallen. St. Loup was in French hands, and Joan's first victory had been won.

Although more than 100 Englishmen died, and even though Joan wore a sword, no one was struck down by her personally. Instead, she seemed deeply grieved by their deaths, even though she had deemed them necessary. She wept over their bodies, wishing that they had just heeded the warnings she'd given them in the name of God. But much more blood would be shed, and this innocent girl would see much more death and gore before Orléans would finally be set free.

* * * *

The victory at St. Loup was just the beginning, the first taste of success for which the French army had been so desperate. The next day, May 5th, was Ascension Day; they celebrated the feast day in rest, but Joan took the opportunity to dictate one last letter to the English. Tying it to an arrow, it was shot into the English ranks. Their response was so derisive and so badly insulted Joan's purity and character that it brought her to tears, but it did not stop her.

On May 6th, the fighting began again as the French gathered themselves to begin an assault in earnest. The eventual goal was simple: to recapture Les Tourelles, the gatehouse that the English had been controlling since the fateful beginning of the siege. To do this, they first had to destroy several English bastilles, such as Boulevart, Augustins, and St. Privé. When the day dawned, the military commanders were aghast to find that the civilians of Orléans had rallied around the white banner of their heroine and formed a makeshift militia that was rich in passion but lamentably low in equipment and training. Nonetheless, Joan persuaded the commanders to let the people join in, and so they sailed across the Loire together, Joan's white stallion being ferried over the river on a boat. The white horse's hooves had barely struck the shore before Joan was swinging its head toward the bastille of Boulevart, shouting for her troops to rally around her. They would have followed her anywhere, and so when she charged Boulevart, to the dismay of the commanders, her people went with her. The move, probably precipitated by one of Joan's voices, was unplanned and dangerous. Charging upon Boulevart, they began to assault the bastille, but their passion quickly faded when cries of dismay were heard. The English were sending reinforcements to Boulevart from St. Privé. Terror seized the French, and they began to fall back, physically pulling Joan's horse with them. What happened next is uncertain, but the only version that legend and history gives us is that the English troops burst out of the bastille to give chase. When Joan saw them coming, she wrenched her horse back around and raised her banner aloft, shouting four words that became her motto, her battle cry, and her personal anthem: *Au Nom de Dieu!* ("In the Name of God!"). She stood alone, her own people fleeing, her enemy charging, and she shouted the words that she believed in, holding up her flag as a symbol of hope and courage. The English, suddenly disconcerted by this turn of events, skidded to a halt. The French rallied, and the assault began afresh.

This time, it was successful. By the end of the day, St. Privé had been evacuated, Boulevart had fallen, and Les Augustins was in the hands of the French. They had torn down every obstacle that stood between them and Les Tourelles. Now it was time to take back their city.

Chapter 10 – A Sign Provided

May 7th, 1429 dawned with hope. The French had made more progress in a single day than they had since the beginning of the siege many months ago. Les Tourelles was within their sight, almost within their grasp. Thanks to the strange young peasant girl, erratic as her actions could be, they were starting to believe that perhaps the siege could be lifted after all.

Joan had proven herself courageous, but she had also been unpredictable, and her wild presence made some of the commanders uncomfortable. What was more, she had obtained a fairly minor but still painful wound in her foot during the fight at Les Augustins, and so the commanders tried to persuade her to stay in Orléans for the final assault. Perhaps Joan considered doing as they asked. She had been in the thick of the fight that day, a fight for which she had received no training or conditioning; she had experienced the mass destruction and thoughtless carnage of real war and even felt what it was like to be injured in it. It was all suddenly very real. Yet even this could not persuade Joan to change any of her convictions: she believed God had told her to lift the siege, and lift it she would, no matter what.

That night, she told one of her close associates, Jean Pasquerel, a friar who served as her confessor, to stay close to her, "for tomorrow I will have much to do and more than I ever had, and tomorrow blood will leave my body above my breast." This ominous prediction didn't seem to have much effect on Joan's determination to join in the coming battle.

The next morning, as the day broke, the French rushed forth. They poured toward the gates of Les Tourelles, bright and swift as the beams of sunlight gushing over the landscape as the sun rose, and it seemed that nothing could stop them; one history describes the zeal of the French soldiers as so powerful that they seemed to "believe themselves immortal." Their eyes fixed on Joan's white banner as she rode out before them, and they launched themselves at Les Tourelles, where they bombarded their enemies for hours upon hours. Cannons cracked, swords clashed, voices screamed, and above it all, the serene white banner of Joan of Arc floated upon the breeze. She was always in the thick of it yet never striking a blow. She didn't need to. Her mere presence, the assurance in her blue eyes, and the rise and fall of her lilting voice calling out her war cry of *Au Nom de Dieu!* was stronger than the sharpest two-edged sword, more powerful than the biggest cannon.

The morning wore on with the French fighting on with strength and perseverance. Their courage somehow found no end, their endurance unabated as their beloved Joan stayed shoulder-to-shoulder with them, crying out encouragements. She would not strike a blow, but she was a weapon in and of herself.

As the sun began to reach its zenith, it happened. The ominous prophecy Joan had made about herself came suddenly and sickeningly true. Jean Pasquerel, as Joan had asked, was right next to her when he heard the twang of an English bowstring. Joan, halfway through helping to prop up a scaling ladder against the wall of the fortress, barely had time to look up before the arrow hit her. The force of it flung her off her feet, cruelly smashing her tiny body against the earth with a dull thud and the ring of armor. Blood spilled upon the ground, and Joan gave a single cry of pain and terror as her banner wobbled for a second and then, its owner torn away from it, fell to the ground.

Pasquerel was beside her almost before he could think. The arrow had pierced her shoulder so deeply that the head of it was protruding from her back, its ugly metal gleaming with wet blood when Pasquerel gently rolled her onto her side. Suddenly, the bright and shining maiden, the leader of an army, the inspiration of the masses, was just a seventeen-year-old girl lying in the dirt and crying as she bled. She was dreadfully, frighteningly human, clinging to Pasquerel's hand, scared and wounded.

Her soldiers were just as shaken, but they rushed to her aid. Carrying her away from the heat of battle, they attempted to do what they could for her. Despite her pain and fear, when a soldier arrived and offered to heal her with witchcraft, Joan immediately refused, stating that she would rather die than sin. Instead, the local healers did what they could. It wasn't much. In the modern era, she would have gone into surgery, been given strong painkillers, and been cleaned and made comfortable. But this was the fifteenth century. Healers had not yet learned to wash their hands. They treated her with cotton, oil, and bacon fat. There was no anesthetic or analgesic as they dragged the arrow from her shoulder.

* * * *

When Joan was carried broken from the battlefield, the hearts of the French soldiers all seemed to go with her, torn and bloodied just as she was. They continued to fight as the day grew longer and longer, but with every hour, they seemed to tire faster. The English, jeering that they had killed the witch, rallied and held their fortress with more confidence. By late afternoon, Dunois had to face the fact that his men were faltering. Promising as their first assault had been, he couldn't deny that they were nothing without Joan.

With a heavy heart, Dunois decided to call off his men and try again the next day. When Joan heard the news, she dragged herself from the place where she was lying. Weak and pale but resolute, she begged Dunois to wait just a few minutes before giving the order. He didn't have the heart to deny her this request. She called for her horse, pulled herself into the saddle, and rode away to a nearby vineyard.

Among these grapevines, Joan sat and prayed. Her white stallion stood over her as if on guard; the gentle spring breeze stirred the deep green of the leaves around her, and the sounds of battle were muffled and distant. She breathed the peace deeply, bowed her head, and focused her every thought on the God she trusted. And she heard the voices.

* * * *

The soldiers couldn't understand why Dunois hadn't called them off yet. What hope did they have? La Pucelle, the Maid who was leading them, had been wounded. Some believed that she must have been killed or she would have been back by now. Had she abandoned them? Had God abandoned them? Every doubt gnawed deeper and deeper into their mental strength, even as every blow, every mine they dug, and every cannon they launched ate away at their physical power. They had been fighting for hours. Dusk was creeping into the western sky, and yet Les Tourelles held, the English somehow seeming invincible. The French didn't want to fight anymore. They just wanted to give up and go home.

Then, they heard it. The pure and piercing voice, rising above the brutal grunts and thuds of the battle.

"*Tout est vostre—et y entrez!*" it cried. "All is yours, go in!"

It was Joan. She came rushing up to them, carrying a scaling ladder despite her wounded arm, and her eyes were lit with hope. Her presence among them ignited them, the glimmer of her shapely armor the spark that they needed to rise into a blazing flame. She flung herself at the walls, her banner held high, shouting for them to join her. The English, who had believed she was dead, faltered. Had this witch risen from the grave, or had she miraculously been raised from the dead? Either way, it was a daunting prospect. They hesitated for just long enough. The French surged into the bastille, forcing the English back. Back to the drawbridge. Back to the last barbican of Les Tourelles. Back from the entire southern bank of the Loire, until every last Englishman had been forced from the Les Tourelles complex, from Orléans itself.

That night, Les Tourelles was retaken by the French. The next morning, the English surrendered. The sign that the examiners at Poitiers had asked for had been provided: somehow, this peasant girl who seemed to be aided by divine grace had arrived in a city on the verge of surrender and in little more than a week brought an impossible victory.

It was official. Joan of Arc was the Maid of Orléans, the heroine that France had been waiting for.

Chapter 11 – The Battle of Patay

French morale had never been higher. It was June 18th, 1429, about six weeks after the wonderful victory at Orléans, and the French had been campaigning throughout the Loire Valley ever since the siege had been lifted. And for the first time in decades, they were winning.

After weeks of attacking English-controlled fortifications, the French had put the English army to flight. Now, spurred onward and commanded by Joan of Arc, the French were pursuing their enemies up an old Roman road toward the town of Patay. Scouts had been sent to search for the English but had not yet returned with word of their whereabouts. In the meantime, the vanguard continued on the road, riding past stands of thick forest and brush. Despite the fact that they knew they were riding through enemy territory and that the surrounding vegetation was so thick that an opposing army could well be concealed nearby, the French moved with confidence. The Maid of Orléans had told them that they would have another victory today, and they believed her. The commanders had asked her where they would find the English, hoping that her saints would have told her. Her answer was cryptic but inspired courage: "Ride boldly on, we will have good guidance."

So now the vanguard of eighty knights, led by La Hire—who had also fought alongside Joan at Orléans—was riding briskly and without fear. Patay was in sight; the English had been fleeing all day, but the French horses were fresh, and their riders spurred them on with a new confidence. Joan, leading the main body of the French army, was right behind them. They believed they had nothing to fear.

They were only a few miles from Patay when the guidance that Joan had prophesied apparently came to their aid. Riding through the countryside, the clatter of the horses' feet and the clang of armor had been spooking small wild creatures all morning. There was a sudden rustle from the woods, then the sound of hooves on the road. Some of the horses were startled, and the knights scrambled to maintain control over them, looking around wildly to see what had just come crashing out of the woods.

It was a stag. Majestic, graceful, it launched itself over the road in flight, its dark eyes wide, its white tail thrown up as it fled. Its legs were thin as shadows but carried it across the ground with breathtaking speed, its spreading antlers thrown back over its shoulders. The knights and horses settled, feeling foolish for being startled by a deer. The stag fled, disappearing into the woods. Then they heard the shouting. Pausing, the knights listened as male voices filled the peaceful countryside, a clamor that could only come from a large group of men. And they were shouting in English. The stag, in its panic, had run directly into the English army, giving away their position.

La Hire quickly discovered that the English were still scrambling to put together their usual defenses—a line of sharpened stakes in front of lines of longbowmen, a formation that had been all but impenetrable to cavalry during the entire war—and called for his cavalry. While messengers raced back to the army to tell them that the English had been found, La Hire called up his men, set them against the English, and charged.

* * * *

Ever since Orléans, the French army had been enjoying victory after victory, and with each fight that they won, the Dauphin was placing more and more trust in the leadership of Joan. When she met with him the day after the English retreated from Orléans, he was a changed man—exuberant with joy and so ecstatic that some chroniclers describe him as having almost kissed her when he saw her, so overwhelmed was he with relief and happiness. Joan had done what no one had thought could be done. She had lifted the siege or, according to her, had been the instrument that God Himself used to lift the siege.

Now the English had been put to flight, and Charles had several options when it came to what to do next. The most sensible thing would be to push for a campaign toward Paris or Normandy, thereby incrementally increasing the territories that he controlled.

But Joan had other ideas. Attending the councils of war when she could, she insisted that their focus needed to be on the next part of the mission that the voices had given her: crowning Charles officially as the king of France. This could only be done in Reims, the city where generations upon generations of kings had held their coronation ceremonies. The difficulty was that Reims was miles and miles into enemy territory, much farther than Paris, and of little strategic significance. Yet Joan was adamant. Her voices had told her to go, and she was determined that she was going.

Having seen what had just come to pass at Orléans, Charles found that he couldn't say no to her. She had to be the saint, the hero, the savior that France had been waiting for. He gave her permission to lead an offensive campaign through the Loire Valley, heading for Reims. Through the beginning of June, Joan rode alongside the Duke of Alençon, who was one of her most fervent supporters especially after she saved his life during a battle at Jargeau by warning him about a cannon that was about to fire at him. The duke jumped out of the way, and another man standing nearby was killed. It awoke a sense of loyalty in Alençon, and he did everything that Joan advised him to do.

It may have seemed a senseless strategy to listen to this uneducated girl, who usually advocated for direct attacks even when faced with unlikely odds, but it worked. In the five days between June 12th and June 17th, the French beat the English army out of the Loire Valley despite reinforcements that had arrived from Paris. First Jargeau, then Meung, and then Beaugency fell before them. Now the English were running north, and the French were hot on their heels, ready for another great victory.

* * * *

La Hire's cavalry charge surged toward the hedgerows where the English archers were concealed. Panicking, the English line started to crumble before the cavalry could even reach it. A scattered volley of arrows sprang forth, bouncing off plate armor, but while one or two knights screamed and fell, the charge continued. Faced with a wall of armored horses barreling toward them, the archers turned tail and fled.

It was not so much a battle as it was a massacre. The English put up almost no resistance. They were cut down as they ran, the panicking army utterly routed, scattering into the countryside. By the time Joan and the main army reached the battlefield, the fighting was mostly over, the entire field strewn with the torn and broken corpses of thousands of Englishmen.

The sight broke Joan's heart even though the English were her enemies. Dismounting from her horse, she knelt down beside the nearest dying English soldier, cradled his head in her hands, and tried her best to soothe him as he faded slowly into death.

Two thousand Englishmen died that day; of the French, only about a hundred fell. It was the humiliating Battle of Agincourt all over again, except this time in reverse. The French had won, and they were determined to keep on winning.

Chapter 12 – Beans for the Apocalypse

Illustration V: Troyes in the modern day

The army that set out from Orléans in late June was completely different than the one Joan had first led out of Chinon. Then, she had just a handful of men, all of them dispirited and barely clinging onto the hope that her white banner had given them. Now, her men numbered as many as twelve thousand. These were knights and common soldiers and even ordinary citizens of the surrounding towns who had armed themselves with swords and spears and mounted their little farm ponies to join the cause. Everyone wanted to follow Joan, wherever she led.

And despite some misgivings from other commanders who believed that the army should turn to Normandy instead, she was leading them to Reims. Charles met the army at Gien the evening after they left Orléans; he was wildly excited, radiant at the prospect of finally being given the crown that he'd been born for. Joan was serene as ever, believing and insisting firmly that they were going to get to Reims and that Charles was going to be crowned, no matter what dared to stand in their way.

As it turned out, not much did stand in their way. The English believed that Joan was a witch, a terrifying sorceress whose curses were invincible; she struck terror into their hearts, and their resistance melted before her, morale plummeting as their commanders desperately tried to keep control over their panicking men. The towns may have been occupied by Englishmen, but they were populated by the French who were willing to ally themselves once again to the Dauphin now that word had it that he was traveling with a bona fide saint. As they moved nearer to Reims, the French army hardly had cause to strike a single blow. City after city flung open their gates and surrendered, welcoming Charles as their king. It was less of a campaign and more of a victory march on the road to Reims.

It was during this time, however, that Joan—for the first and possibly last time—performed an act of violence. On June 29th, as the army headed out of Gien to start its march, Joan noticed a group of young women hanging around the gates of the city. In an age where thousands of men were torn away from their wives and families and spent weeks or months on the road, unaccompanied and often bored, prostitution flourished. Wherever the army went, prostitutes went with it, always on the edges of the camp, and this day was no exception. As the army left Gien, Joan saw that some of the young men had noticed the prostitutes. They headed toward them, utterly distracted from their mission, and Joan flew into a rage. Charging toward them on her horse, she ripped out her sword. Terrified by the wrath of their leader, the men scrambled away, the prostitutes fleeing, but they were too slow for Joan. Ignoring the prostitutes, she set furiously upon the men, slapping them with the flat of her sword. They were safe from any cuts by the edge, but the flat was hard enough, and Joan swung it with a strength born of fury. She was only about five feet tall, yet she struck the nearest soldier hard enough that the sword broke.

The soldiers thus chastised, Joan returned to the head of the army, sweaty and wild-eyed with anger. No man even dared to look at a prostitute as they headed off on their march. One of their first stops, the town of Auxerre, was familiar to Joan; she had visited it on her journey from Vaucouleurs to Chinon, sneaking inside the city walls in order to hear Mass. Now, she rode boldly toward it at the head of a victorious army. While Auxerre remained loyal to its fealty of the Duke of Burgundy, it did not resist the French, instead supplying the army with provisions; after a brief rest, they continued toward a city that must have held considerable heartache for Charles: Troyes.

* * * *

It was in Troyes that Charles's own mother had signed off his birthright, giving away the country to an English king. Bitterness must have filled Charles's heart as they neared the city. If only Isabeau had not signed that treaty, Charles would have been king by now—a king at war, certainly, but at least a true and official king. He would not have had to fight tooth and nail across his own country just to be able to wear the crown that he believed he'd been born for.

Yet here he was, approaching Troyes itself with a vast force of loyal soldiers, led by this strange and yet undeniably charismatic young woman. Joan rode beside the king, now on a black charger; the white banner flapped above her head which bore a short and boyish haircut, still growing out after she had been disguised as a man for the journey to Chinon. It was early morning when Troyes came into view, and it was immediately obvious that this was the first city that would not be going down without a fight. Even though the garrison at Troyes numbered only 500 men, they sallied out courageously against Charles's huge force. After a brief but intense fight, they were driven back into Troyes. Little or no damage was done to the French army, but the facts were clear: Troyes was going to resist.

The city that had disinherited Charles would now continue to be a thorn in his side. Confident that it wouldn't be long before Troyes submitted, Charles ordered his men to dig in and prepare for a siege. The Anglo-Burgundian garrison was vastly outnumbered, and Charles was sure it wouldn't be long before they gave up.

There was just one problem: The French army had nothing to eat. The supplies they had bought at Auxerre were long gone; now, they found themselves camping in the countryside, deep into enemy territory, with thousands of human and equine mouths to feed. Summertime allowed for the horses to graze, but the army was made up of finicky French knights who were used to luxurious cuisine.

The solution to this issue was, like Joan of Arc herself, about as strange and unorthodox as they came. The previous winter, a wandering friar had made his way into Troyes. His message was that the end of the world was at hand, that Jesus was coming back that summer, and that the people of Troyes needed to be ready to feed an angelic host. For that reason, instead of planting the usual wheat crop, the farmers of Troyes and its surroundings had planted all of their fields with an early crop of beans.

No angelic army descended upon Troyes as Brother Richard had promised. But there was an army, and it was hungry, and it arrived just as the beans began to ripen.

* * * *

Troyes continued to hold out stubbornly for several days as the French army surrounded the city. Charles began to wonder if besieging the city was really worth his while; their aim was to reach Reims, not to capture everything in their path. He started to discuss his options with his commanders, most of whom were in favor of retreating and going back to Gien instead. One of the older men finally succeeded in persuading them to consult with Joan before making any decisions, considering that they had followed Joan this far.

Her response was predictable. She believed that Troyes was going to fall soon, within the next couple of days, and Charles just had to stand his ground. Just as she had asked Robert de Baudricourt to tell Charles that he had to stand firm against his enemies, long before the name of Jeanne d'Arc meant anything to anyone in France, now she was continuing to exhort the Dauphin to be brave and persevere.

Gathering the army, Joan ordered the soldiers to start building outworks in the moat of Troyes, preparing for a full-scale offensive. Her white banner had given them victory before; they trusted that it would do so again, and they worked fervently and fearlessly.

The Anglo-Burgundians inside Troyes had already heard all the stories about the witch of Orléans and her terrifying powers. They watched in dismay as Joan's outworks took shape and saw, with horror, that she had arrayed them in as skillful a manner as would any experienced military commander. Her apparent supernatural powers frightened them, and they hurriedly sent forth some of the city's leaders to attempt peaceful negotiations with the French army.

Among these was that same Brother Richard whose preaching had furnished the Frenchmen with their beans. Although he was suspicious of Joan at first, fearfully sprinkling holy water at her to ward off her demons, he would later become one of her allies. Nonetheless, despite the friar's misgivings, an agreement was reached allowing the garrison to escape and surrender the city. Later that morning, the gates of Troyes were thrown wide open. And the

Dauphin Charles, overjoyed and triumphant, could enter at last the city where his own family had betrayed him.

Chapter 13 – The French King Crowned

Illustration VI: Joan of Arc at the Coronation of King Charles VII *by Jean Auguste Dominique Ingres, 1854. The clergyman depicted is Jean Pasquerel, Joan's companion.*

Reims Cathedral, July 17th,1429. It was here that the first king of France—then king of the Franks—had been baptized by Saint Remi almost a thousand years ago. And ever since then, for generation upon generation, every king of France had been crowned here in a ceremony as ancient as it was holy and as venerated as it was elaborate. The vaulted ceilings rose up into the sky, the walls gilded and lavishly decorated in a show of shameless splendor, and below the towering height of the roof stood some of the highest-ranking people in all of France, most notably, the young king who knelt by the altar, ready to receive his crown at last.

And among them all was Joan of Arc, a peasant girl from the borders of Lorraine. A nobody, and yet her name was on the lips of every man in France and England alike. She could neither read nor write, she had no schooling, and she was one of the most low-born people in the entire country. And yet here she stood, not only an onlooker at the coronation of the king of France but an instrumental part of the events that had led up to this very moment. She had shed her fair share of blood, sweat, and tears to bring Charles to Reims, and now she watched in glowing satisfaction and joy as the ceremony took place.

The coronation ceremony was an elaborate one. One of its key components was a vial of holy oil, said to have been brought to Saint Remi for the baptism of Clovis I by a dove descended from heaven. The oil was housed in a pure golden reliquary, which contained a crystal vial, and it was used sparingly and reverently upon Charles's back and shoulders just as it had been used on all of his ancestors that had been king. Then, the constable of France entered, bearing a royal and elaborately carved sword that was used symbolically to knight the king. This particular sword, often since known as the Sword of the Maid in honor of Joan, has since been lost to time; it vanished somewhere during the French Revolution many years later. The king was then awarded his golden spurs, a sword, his royal robes, ring and scepter, and finally, the crown of France. At last, the bejeweled crown was lowered onto the head of the Dauphin Charles. He was Dauphin no longer. He was the king.

Throughout the ceremony—which lasted about five hours—Joan had been standing motionless near the king, watching in contented silence and holding her banner. It was a tattered thing by now, worn throughout the many battles, but the hope it held still beat hard in the hearts of every Frenchman as they finally beheld their king upon the throne. Joan herself didn't move until the king was finally crowned. Then her restraint seemed to have left her. She threw aside her banner and flung herself at Charles's feet, just as she had done months ago when she identified the king among three hundred courtiers. "Noble king!" she cried out, addressing him as "king" for the first time since that first meeting. "Now is accomplished the will of God, who wished me to lift the siege of Orléans." She was crying openly, tears streaming down her cheeks as she clung to Charles's legs. With the emotion running as high as it was inside the cathedral, it was the last straw. The bystanders broke down into tears as Joan clung to the feet of her king and rejoiced. She had done what her voices had told her to do. She had brought the king to Reims.

With that, the ceremony was closed by a fanfare of trumpets. The trumpet players were so filled with emotion that their fanfare seemed to rock the very cathedral; in the words of one of the witnesses, "it seemed the vaults of the church must be riven apart."

* * * *

Reims had capitulated to the approaching French army, throwing open its gates without any resistance and welcoming the Dauphin inside for his coronation. Now that he was crowned King Charles VII, the king knew that his work was far from done. France was still in a state of civil war, and the English were everywhere, especially swarming over his capital—Paris.

Joan wasn't done with the war, either. Despite the fact that the battles seemed to have had a profound emotional effect on her, she was ready for more. Soon after the coronation, she informed the king that her voices had instructed her to take the army and head directly to Paris for an assault that aimed to retake the city. The Duke of

Alençon predictably supported her in this decision, but Charles was not so easily persuaded. Even after the victories that Joan had brought them, part of him seemed to remain a little suspicious. He refused to follow her blindly and instead called a council to discuss what to do next, where it was decided that it would be a wiser move to attempt to negotiate a truce with the Duke of Burgundy, still a key ally for the English.

In the meantime, Joan stayed in Reims, having little to do but still being of importance to the people. After four months of constant activity, it must have been a relief to have some respite and stay in one city for more than a few weeks. And it must have been a strange new world for this peasant girl who had never been in contact with the higher classes outside of the military. She was one of the most famous—and also the most powerful, considering that most of the French soldiers would have followed her anywhere, even if it was against their commanders' orders—people in France, and yet none of it seemed to affect her behavior. She refused to indulge in the luxuries that were available to her in Reims, often refusing even to eat meat or vegetables. Instead, Joan often opted to have only a little bread, perhaps longing for the simple diet that she had once had when she was just an ordinary young girl in Domrémy. She often said since the beginning of her rise that if it was up to her, she would have stayed behind in the village. She had a far greater desire to tend sheep and spin wool than to lead armies and crown kings. Yet her voices compelled her; she insisted that the saints were telling her what to do, and Joan lived to obey their orders.

Yet this time, Charles would not be convinced to march directly on Paris. Instead, he was negotiating with Philip of Burgundy, ignoring Joan and her voices. It would turn out to be a terrible mistake.

Chapter 14 – The Siege of Paris

Illustration VII: Joan at the Siege of Paris

While Joan continued to urge the newly-crowned King Charles VII to attack Paris without delay, the king dug in his toes. He refused to move on Paris until he had finished his negotiations with the Duke of

Burgundy, no matter how earnest Joan pleaded with him to heed her words. It would have been easy after all that Joan had achieved during her time with the army to feel betrayed and affronted by Charles's lack of trust in her, but if she did, she didn't show it. Instead, she accompanied her friend the Duke of Alençon on an almost aimless march, capturing towns surrounding Reims. Most of these surrendered without any resistance.

Meanwhile, as Charles attempted to reach some kind of pact with Philip, the deceitful Duke of Burgundy was only participating in negotiations because he was playing for time. Even as he smiled and nodded in his meetings with the French, even as he played friendly on the surface, Philip was busy giving orders to his men to have Paris fortified against a potential attack from the French. He only ceased negotiations when his fortifications were finished. The entire exercise had been utterly fruitless; instead of coming close to peace, Charles had succeeded only in giving his enemy the upper hand. He would have done well to heed Joan's words. Yet he didn't. And for that, the French army would pay the price.

* * * *

It was late August before the negotiations finally came to an end, and Charles decided that an attack on Paris would be necessary after all. Joan and the rest of the army had been moving across the country toward the capital, and on August 26th, 1429, she and her men captured a small village near Paris and established themselves and their troops at La Chapelle. Here, they started sending small groups to the city to reconnoiter the gates and determine just how much Philip had been able to improve the defenses.

What they saw brought them great dismay. Paris had been founded centuries ago, at the end of the third century BCE, and over the passage of more than a millennium, it had only grown in importance and strength. The fortress was already almost impregnable before the Duke of Burgundy started to fortify it against the attack that Joan now found herself leading. Now, it was an intimidating sight, even though Joan and other commanders knew its garrison only held about 3,000 men. Charles's army numbered 10,000, but they did not have the advantage of the strong defenses that stood guard all around the heart of the city.

Joan headed off to a small chapel at La Chapelle, known as St. Genevieve's Chapel, a few days after their arrival in the area. Her purpose was to pray, and it is easy to see why she chose to seek her divine inspiration from Saint Genevieve. Born more than a thousand years before, she had also been a virgin saint, a woman who had traveled all over the country preaching and healing. St. Genevieve, too, had claimed to have seen visions of saints and angels, perhaps even in a similar way to how Joan had seen them. She must have felt like the only person in the world with whom Joan could identify with, as Joan's voices continued to speak to her, urging her to get to Paris and to take France back for its rightful and recently anointed king. Joan knelt down there in the peace of the little chapel, and she prayed, hoping that her voices would return to guide her.

That same chapel still stands today, although Paris's streets have grown and swollen so much that it is now a part of Paris itself. The very spot where Joan knelt in prayer can still be visited today. As the sun set, Joan took her place, and as the night wore on, she didn't move, staying there, her entire mind focused on listening for her voices. It was dawn, and her body was cold, stiff, and aching when she arose from her knees, but Joan was filled with determination. They were going to take Paris, and she was going to lead her army forward to victory once again.

Charles only reached Paris on September 7th, having been wasting his time once again in an agony of indecision. As soon as he arrived with some reinforcements, Joan and the Duke of Alençon gave the order to attack. Joan herself rode at the head of the army. The Anglo-Burgundians watched in trepidation as she came into view, a feminine figure clad in gleaming steel, astride a black stallion that flashed in the noonday sun. A breeze unfurled her banner above her head; pure white against a landscape ablaze with the warm colors of autumn, it was a symbol of hope for the French, and a thing of terror for all who stood against them.

This time there would be no attempts to hold Joan back. The commanders knew that their men fought best if the Maid of Orléans was at their head.

And at the lead Joan was. Seizing her banner, she called up the men. They burst forward, rushing toward the walls of Paris with unrelenting zeal. Joan was at the very front of the army, her banner leading the way as they charged the moat. The air was filled with the crack and thunder of the culverins—medieval cannons—mounted on the nearby buttes; for every volley that France fired, the Parisians returned, raining stone missiles down onto Joan's men. Crossbows twanged, their heavy bolts pouring into the ranks; swords clashed as they threw grappling hooks up the walls and started climbing, fighting hard to prevent being cut down. It was a chaos of death and destruction, but according to one eyewitness named Perceval de Cagny, not a single one of Joan's men was severely wounded, even though many were struck down by cannonballs.

Yet the Parisians did not back down, and the fortifications of the great city held firm. Hour after hour, Joan's men strove against the defenses, and many times they came perilously close to overrunning them entirely, but each time the Parisians managed to push them back. The sun slipped low in the sky, bathing the fighters first in gold, then in twilight as dusk settled over the landscape. Throughout it all, Joan did not waver. She stood upon the outworks, her banner held high, and called them forward with the voice they had followed so many times to victory.

With her white banner flying so proudly, she made a perfect target. A Parisian crossbowman took careful aim at her, hefting the heavy crossbow upon his shoulder. Then he took fire. The bolt sang through the air, an ugly, heavy thing, deadly and brutal in its simplicity. There was a butcher's noise, a slicing of flesh, and Joan collapsed. The bolt had pierced her thigh. She crumpled to the earth, blood bursting out from the jagged wound in her leg from the crossbow bolt jutting cruelly from her young flesh. Crying out in pain, she still somehow managed to struggle into a sitting position. She saw that her soldiers had faltered, and even as she clutched her wound and felt her own warm blood sliding between her fingers, she knew she had to call back the hope that was in them. Raising her voice, she continued to urge them forward, and they renewed the assault.

It wasn't long, however, before Charles decided that the fighting was fruitless. The men had been striving against Paris's defenses for hours, and they were exhausted. He ordered a retreat. Joan had to be bodily carried from the battlefield as she cried that her voices had told her to continue the assault.

The next day, Joan, lying in her bed at La Chapelle with her leg bound up, told Charles that if he attacked Paris again today, the city would be his. But Charles had found her a lot easier to believe in when she was an armored maiden on a horse, not this pale and injured girl lying in a sickbed. He called off the attack. The Siege of Paris was declared a failure, and it became the first defeat that the French would suffer since Joan of Arc joined their ranks.

Chapter 15 – Peace

The defeat at Paris seemed to leach all of the fire and energy back out of King Charles once more. Even though victory seemed to be so close, he had to face one undeniable fact: he couldn't afford to pay his troops. The towns they had captured had only just started to pay taxes once again; the huge army that Charles had amassed in order to get to Reims now needed to be paid, and his coffers were empty after years of collecting taxes from almost only Bourges. Instead, Charles had to disband most of the army, sending many of his soldiers back home.

Winter was fast approaching. As Joan recuperated from the wound she had received at Paris, the leaves fell from the trees, and the first frost started to nip at the landscape at night. So, too, did the bloom of Joan's power begin to fade. Even though her voices reportedly never left her, Charles's confidence did. He was no longer the desperate "King of Bourges" that Joan had met in Chinon more than six months ago. No, he was king now, a king who had received the holy anointing and conquered more territory in three months than France had been able to reclaim in years of war. Suddenly, Joan was no longer needed.

It can't be said that Charles mistreated her during this time. He seemed almost anxious for her to be happy, supplying her with luxury upon luxury, an opulent existence that would have been almost incomprehensible for this ordinary farm girl who had grown up among peasants. Joan's family had been considered wealthy because they always had something on the table for dinner; many of the people that she grew up with had gone to bed hungry, so those who were considered to be well-off simply had their needs supplied. There was room for joy and fun, but there was absolutely none for excess or luxury in their simple lives. Yet now Joan found herself residing in a vast mansion, waited on hand and foot by ladies who were much higher-born than herself. She was given flamboyant clothes to wear and offered the best delicacies that Charles could find to eat. A golden mantle was made for her to be worn over her battle-stained armor. But none of this was what Joan wanted. Her heart yearned for just one thing—to honor the voices. And they told her to go out and defeat the enemy that still controlled the majority of France.

For Charles and his advisers, however, the decision was final. They had believed in Joan when they had no other option, but now that they felt fairly secure in their position, they would no longer place any faith in her. Never again would Jeanne d'Arc ride at the very head of the army. Instead, she could lead small bands on occasional skirmishes, usually only against the bandits and freebooters that plagued France now that an entire army had suddenly found itself with nothing to do. While Charles negotiated truces with the Dukes of Burgundy and Bedford, Joan felt cooped up, trapped, and cornered without any way to obey the saints that she believed were guiding her. One historian chose to use the words "mortal languishment" to describe her condition, and they were likely accurate.

Some of her allies, however, did make an effort to help her. The Duke of Alençon attempted to arrange a campaign into Normandy, but Charles absolutely refused to allow Joan to accompany him. Disheartened, the duke disbanded his troops. It was, eventually, Charles himself that would allow Joan back onto the battlefield once more. Regardless of how much pain and worry he had put Joan through by keeping her with his court, it appears that Charles did care for her welfare, and he finally had to face the fact that keeping Joan off the battlefield may be protecting her body, but it was breaking her heart. He allowed her to join a small campaign that was touring France and subduing the little towns that were left within Charles's territory that had not yet surrendered.

One of these was the town of St. Pierre-le-Moutier. It was a small town, but when Joan reached it with a long-time friend and military commander named Jean d'Aulon commanding her troops, it immediately put up a strenuous resistance. Joan's little army attacked, urged on by the Maiden who was adamant that the city was going to fall. Yet it appeared that this battle would be a hideous echo of what had happened at Paris. The assault was a disaster. D'Aulon sounded the retreat, pulling his troops back to safety; he himself was wounded, and so were many of his men. He was struggling to retreat on an injured leg when he noticed, to his horror, that Joan had not heeded the order. Instead, she stood against the bombardment of the defenders almost alone, only half a dozen courageous men holding their ground beside her.

D'Aulon had been personally charged by the king not to allow anything to happen to Joan, so he couldn't leave her behind. Hurrying toward her, he shouted out, thinking that perhaps she hadn't heard the order. "Jeanne, withdraw, withdraw!" he bellowed as his army stampeded into the distance in wild panic. "You are alone!"

Joan's face was radiant as she turned toward him, as if bathed in heavenly light. That otherworldly glow was in her blue eyes again as she spoke. "I still have with me fifty thousand men!" she called, her laughter filled with confidence. "To work, to work!" Her raised voice rang across the countryside. Its clear tone seemed to wake the retreating army from its fervent panic, and as d'Aulon worked together with Joan to rally the men, they pulled themselves together and renewed the attack. When St. Pierre-le-Moutier finally fell after the second attack, it must have felt like redemption to Joan after the failure at Paris. It did lead many of her contemporaries—and historians—to question whether Paris might have fallen if Joan had those extra few hours she asked for.

Either way, St. Pierre-le-Moutier was to be Joan's last great victory. Peace was starting to descend upon France, a time of relative ease and respite for the people. But for Joan, her glory days had ended. Her suffering was just beginning.

Chapter 16 – Capture

The treaty that Charles had succeeded in negotiating with the Burgundians was short-lived. By the spring of 1430, the fragile peace had disintegrated, and Burgundian soldiers began to march upon French towns once more. The Duke of Burgundy's plan was to seize the towns and cities along the Oise River, thereby protecting Paris from another attempt by the French army—he knew that the city had come perilously close to falling.

One of these towns, and one of the first that he planned to besiege, was Compiègne. It was a small town and not thoroughly fortified, but its inhabitants had declared their loyalty to King Charles VII shortly after his coronation; now, the Duke of Burgundy was determined to reclaim it. He issued a letter to the town's garrison, giving them a harsh reminder that, legally, the city belonged to him. It was not an empty threat, but it was a threat that did not intimidate the citizens of Compiègne. Instead of submitting to the Duke of Burgundy, they prepared for war.

Joan knew as early as March 1430 that danger awaited Compiègne; whether she had been told about it by her voices or learned about it by more earthly means remains unclear. Either way, she knew that she had to do something. Charles refused to give her any troops to command; it was a sad thing for a woman who had once led the entire army, but it seemed that Charles was content with the victories they had won and had no desire to gamble any more of his power on Joan and her visions. But she was far from powerless. She remained one of the most famous women of the era, and the Frenchmen would rally around her, king or no king. By April, she had put together several hundred men and led them to Compiègne in early May—probably without the king's knowledge.

For three weeks, Joan resided in the city, relishing her newfound freedom. Even though she had always honored Charles as her king, even when he was not king yet, her obedience to her voices was more important to her than anything else. At any rate, Charles had not tried to stop her. Perhaps he believed that she was comparatively safe in Compiègne, although he did send some reinforcements there, so it was evident that he knew Burgundy would attack the city.

The Burgundian troops had already been encamped around the city when Joan and her troops got there. They had slipped past under cover of darkness, and as the weeks passed, the Burgundians continued to tighten the noose. All the while, Joan and the commander of the city—Guillaume de Flavy—were working together on a plan to free Compiègne. It involved a sortie against the Burgundian camps with the plan to retreat back into Compiègne if needed, but the goal was to put the Burgundians to flight so that a retreat would not be necessary.

The plan was put into action on May 24th. Joan led the army out in the late afternoon, a dazzling and resplendent figure all aglitter in her golden doublet, the edges of it flowing over the haunches of her stallion as her cavalry galloped after her toward the first of the camps. But there was trouble brewing. An English force had arrived to assist Burgundy, and it was heading rapidly toward the city, toward Joan and her little army.

Back at the raised road that led back into Compiègne, Guillaume de Flavy and his men were charged with protecting the road to ensure that the cavalry could safely retreat if it was needed. They watched with trepidation as Joan led her charge. Thundering into the ranks of the Burgundians, led by that white banner, the French slammed into their enemies; from the boulevard near the city walls, cannons cried out, their loud crack filling the sweet spring air, and the arriving English were thrown back by heavy fire.

But so was Joan. Her cavalry was pushed back and forced to retreat a short distance to regroup. Several of her men glanced back to the inviting open road back to the city, guarded by a lowered drawbridge and a raised portcullis. But Joan soon put any thoughts of retreat out of their minds. Calling out that victory was sure, she brandished her banner and set spurs to her horse. They renewed their charge, crashed into the Burgundians, and this time, they were victorious.

However, as the first line of Burgundians cracked, another camp was galloping to their aid. Joan swung her cavalry around just in time to face them. She and her men found themselves hard-pressed on both sides, struggling viciously against their attackers; Joan was always in the thick of it, never striking a blow but always holding up her banner and shouting out encouragements to any who could hear her.

Yet this time, it wasn't enough. The English reinforcements were starting to break through. Wave after wave of enemies rushed down upon Joan's soldiers, and their courage began to fail them faced with such an overwhelming number of enemies. They were vastly outnumbered, and Joan saw it. She stayed calm, rallying her men with shouts of encouragement, knowing that her plan had allowed for a retreat if necessary. She ordered the retreat, and her men swung their horses about and kicked them on toward home. The horses didn't need to be told twice. They rushed back toward Compiègne, all except for Joan's stallion. Held back, he fought and plunged, wanting to follow his allies, yet Joan held him in, her banner snapping above her head, her only protection. She only let him go once every last one of her surviving men had torn themselves away from the battle. Then she followed at the very rear of her troops, keeping herself between them and the enemy, just as she had always been at the forefront of every charge.

They galloped toward Compiègne, their horses' hooves ringing on the raised road. It was so close. Safety was only a tantalizing few yards away, with the first of Joan's men already reaching the drawbridge. She herself was on the road, crossing the bridge, when Guillaume de Flavy screamed out an order to close the drawbridge. The Burgundians were hot on the heels of the French, and he believed that closing the city was the only way to save it. Or perhaps his treachery was intentional; the real story behind his actions has been lost to time. Yet either way, we know one thing. The drawbridge slammed shut. The portcullis fell to the earth. And Joan of Arc, the heroine of France, was trapped. Behind her, she had a horde of furious enemies determined to take down this witch, and in front, a door shut to her by her own friends.

A handful of Joan's own personal guard had stayed near her, and now they turned to face the mass of Burgundians bearing down upon them. It was a fight that they knew they would lose, even as they knew they had no choice but to fight it. One by one, they were sliced down, butchered by their enemies, until only Joan was left. She wheeled her horse around, trying to find a way to safety, yet there was none. It was a rough Burgundian archer who reached her first, a leering man, his face twisted with hatred at the sight of this woman who had done what nobody else had been able to do. Before Joan could get away, he seized her glittering golden doublet and yanked. She was ripped from the saddle and slammed into the earth, her armor dented and stained with dust, the breath knocked from her where she fell.

* * * *

Joan had little choice other than to surrender. She was immediately captured and dragged from the battlefield by her enemies. While Compiègne had been defended and was safe from Burgundy for the time being, the battle could hardly be considered a victory. The greatest weapon France had had throughout the Hundred Years' War, one of the most unique, most unlikely, and yet most successful military commanders it had ever known had been lost. She was gone, carried off into captivity, lost to France. And it would not be long before she was lost to this world, too.

Chapter 17 – Captive

Joan was carried off to the nearby castle of Beaurevoir where she was to begin her long captivity. It was not an unexpected thing for her. As early as the beginning of April, she testified that St. Catherine and St. Margaret had visited her and told her that she would soon be captured and forced to endure a long and unhappy imprisonment. Joan begged them to make it otherwise, to allow her to be killed in battle rather than face being trapped in some enemy fortress, but the voices were unrelenting. God would help her, they said, but there was no other way. She was going to become a prisoner.

And now, a prisoner she was—perhaps the most valuable prisoner in the history of the Hundred Years' War, even though kings and princes had found themselves behind bars at some point during its sad and difficult course. Valuable as she was, however, she was not treated well. Decades ago, King John II of France had been imprisoned in England; he had been given a luxurious life with court musicians and a comfortable home to call his own. None of these privileges were afforded to Joan. She had long been viewed with extreme suspicion, and now that she was in the hands of her enemies, they were not going to treat her with anything other than the harshness they felt became a sorceress.

It is a sad and bitter fact that Joan had no hope of rescue. She had effectively changed Charles from a hopeless Dauphin, on the verge of fleeing to Scotland to live a life in disgraced exile, to the King of France who commanded an army and controlled much of his country once more, yet no help would come to her from that quarter. Charles heard of her capture and all but dismissed her. He wrote a few threatening letters to England and Burgundy during Joan's captivity, yet he took no action. There was no attempt to ransom her, and Charles did not rally his army and attempt to take the castle where she was being kept. His actions smack of abandonment; his attitude, of ingratitude.

Meanwhile, Joan was stuck in the tower of Beaurevoir, constantly attended by a male guard. This immediately started to pose a problem. Much as Joan conducted herself with modesty to all accounts, she was still a woman—a young, beautiful, and shapely woman, and she started to attract unwanted attention almost at once. It is difficult to comprehend exactly how hard this treatment must have been for Joan. She had grown up in a little village that prided itself on its Catholic faith, a place made up of farmers and merchants who knew each other and had known each other for generations, a place too small for scandal. Then she had been the Maid, the virgin who was to save the kingdom, revered and always treated with respect. Now she was just a prisoner, and she found herself having to fight off the lewd advances of her guards and visitors, trying her hardest to keep herself pure the way she had vowed to her God that she would.

In her desperation, Joan turned to the same defense that she had employed on her journey to Chinon: men's clothing. The tight hosen of the era, tucked into boots, was at least some protection against those who would think to rape her. Even though her captors often tried to persuade her otherwise, she refused to wear a woman's dress.

In an era when women were never seen wearing any kind of pants, it was scandalous, strange, and even—in some eyes—an act of sin. Yet to Joan, it was a panicking bid to maintain her purity.

Between her fear for her virginity and her worry over how things were faring in the rest of France, Joan was driven to extreme lengths in her attempts to escape from Beaurevoir. Her first attempt was made as early as June 6th, when she succeeded in slamming the door on her guard in the tower and tried to flee. Her plan was thwarted when a porter happened upon her at that moment and managed to recapture her.

Her next and most dangerous attempt came in October, shortly after a visit from one ribald knight who did his best to molest her.

* * * *

The very tower where Joan had tried to lock her guard away was her prison. She was allowed only one small liberty: to walk around the very top of the tower and look out over the countryside from between the battlements. It was more than sixty feet off the ground, and there was no way down: just the sheer drop of the walls down to the rocky ground below. One morning, as Joan stood in the chill autumn air, she stared down at the drop, and a thought filled her mind.

Even now, abandoned and imprisoned, Joan had no intentions of taking her own life. But a wild hope began to beat in her breast. If she, a peasant girl, could lift in only days a siege that had endured for three-quarters of a year, surely escaping from this tower was not an impossible miracle. She walked over to the battlements and stepped up onto the low wall, keeping her hands braced against the battlements on either side of her. The drop gaped below her yet failed to frighten her. Perhaps if she jumped, she could run, disappear into the countryside, and find her way back to her men.

Later, Joan would tell how her voices had arrived at that moment and begged her not to jump, urging her that it was not God's will.

But this was the one time when she would choose to ignore them. Joan jumped. The wind howled against her, snagging at her growing hair, screaming in her ears as the ground rushed up closer and closer—

She struck the ground with a force that rendered her senseless. The impact should have killed her. Instead, Joan escaped with only a concussion and some scrapes and bruises; every bone in her body was still thoroughly intact.

* * * *

In November 1430, shortly after her escape attempt, Joan was sold like a piece of furniture. The Burgundians were still allied with the English, and after months of negotiations, they agreed to sell her to their English friends for the sum of 10,000 *livres tournois*. She was shipped unceremoniously to Rouen at the end of December, then an English-held fortress in France, and here her captivity began to take a turn for the worse.

While she was kept in a tower cell instead of the dungeon, Joan still had to contend with cold, darkness, damp, and pests—and these were not only in the form of rats. The English guards were even worse than the Burgundians. Joan was terrified of them, and to make matters worse, there was no walking about freely in Rouen as there had been in Beaurevoir. Perhaps because of her escape attempts, Joan was now kept not only in a cell but in chains. Her legs were shackled then chained to one another and to her bed; the chains were so tight that she could not walk without assistance. For a young woman who had never known anything but freedom, this treatment must have been utterly intolerable. She had grown up running through the fields of Domrémy then lived at the forefront of Charles's army, riding a stallion across the vastness of France; yet now it was a like a punishment to move just from her bed to the cell next door, which served as her crude and stinking toilet.

To make matters worse, the English, despite all of their laws, were determined to persecute Joan to every length they could find. Female prisoners were usually kept in a convent instead of a cell, where they were guarded by nuns and usually never shackled. Prisoners-of-war, on the other hand, were treated as roughly as Joan was. Yet at least prisoners-of-war had the faint hope of release once the war was over.

There would be none of this hope for Joan. Shortly after her arrival in Rouen, it became evident that the English had no intentions of ever setting her free. They were going to have her stand trial. And they were going to execute her, whether the trial was fair or not.

Chapter 18 – A Saint Tried for Heresy

Illustration VIII: Joan's interrogation by the Cardinal of Winchester
Everything about Joan's trial was unfair and unjust.

For a start, there were no grounds on which to start an ecclesiastical trial. Much of her trial was recorded, and the documents concerning it have been studied extensively by all kinds of experts over the centuries, and yet none of them could find evidence that would—in the laws of that era—justify the decision to put her on trial. She was put on trial anyway, and it was obvious at once that this was no real trial. It was simply an attempt to discredit Joan as much as possible before her inevitable execution.

The court that was assembled to try Joan consisted almost entirely of Englishmen, Burgundians, and their sympathizers. Those who would dare to question the trial's agenda were secretly threatened with death if they refused to comply. To make matters worse, many of the documents involved in Joan's trial were falsified to ensure that she couldn't win. And the last blow was to refuse Joan any form of legal representation. She represented herself. She had no choice.

Yet it would soon become obvious to Joan's captors that this was not as much of a problem for her as they expected it would be. The Maid of France was about to astonish everyone around her one more time. One last time.

* * * *February 21st, 1431. It was only a couple of months since Joan had been brought to Rouen, and already she found herself before the court, facing a roomful of enemies with not a single friend to come to her aid. She had been abandoned by everyone—everyone but her voices, and yet somehow, they seemed to be enough for her. She walked into the room utterly collected, and that was the first thing that unnerved the court. They had likely never actually seen Joan in their lives; they expected some shivering wreck, some scared and trembling wisp of a girl who had only clueless and stumbling answers. She was an illiterate peasant, after all.

Instead, walking into the room, Joan bore herself with the humility of a saint but the confidence of a queen. She gave the room a single steady glance with her strange blue eyes, and at once they could see that she was unafraid. To make matters worse, they knew—although likely she didn't—that a preliminary inquiry had already been conducted and people from her past were interviewed to establish her character. No one had been able to say anything against her, so the English knew that they were going to have their work cut out for them in order to find any kind of justification for her death.

Bishop Pierre Cauchon put the first question to Joan, a routine one concerning the oath under which she would testify. "Do you swear to speak the truth in answer to such questions as are put to you?" he asked.

Joan regarded him with a steely eye. He had expected her to meekly mumble a yes. Instead, her answer was as fearless as the one during the examination at Poitiers. "I do not know what you wish to examine me on," she said calmly, knowing full well that no one could really prove why she was on trial. "Perhaps you might ask such things that I would not tell."

This would set the tone for all of Joan's answers during the trial. She refused to accept the oath, and accordingly, she refused to give whole answers for much of the trial as well. Concerning her saints and voices, she would describe who they were and what they had said with clarity, but she refused to go into too much detail about their appearance, saying that she didn't have leave to reveal everything about them. As for her audience with Charles, she absolutely refused to share the confidential details of their first meeting. "Ask him," she told the court boldly.

But there would be no asking Charles. Charles would have none of the trial. Joan was alone before some of the most prestigious theologians in the known world, and yet she was absolutely undaunted.

On the first day of her trial, her prosecutors told her that if she made any further attempts to escape from Rouen—as she had continued to try, undeterred by her near-death experience at Beaurevoir—she would immediately be convicted of heresy. Joan rejected this statement at once, knowing that it was unlawful. She would continue to refuse to swear to tell the truth in all things, although she was forthcoming with a lot of information about the voices.

For the next several days, Joan would be questioned every day in something that resembled an interrogation more than it did a trial. Every day she would spar with the court about the oath, and every day the court would try a new angle to prove that her voices were nothing other than a hallucination, a psychological manifestation of a physiological quirk that came about as a result of her habits or health. To this day, though many experts in the medical field have studied her case, it still cannot be said where these voices came from. She was far too robust to have suffered from one of the typical diseases of the period and far too lucid to have had a recognizable mental illness.

Joan testified that the voices were still with her and that one had spoken to her on the very day of one of her sessions, telling her to "Answer boldly; God will help thee." And boldly she did answer, sometimes sassing her questioners by telling them that she had nothing to say to them or otherwise describing events or visions with a clarity and calmness that nobody could have expected. She was questioned on every aspect of her life, from the prophecies surrounding her to the visions she experienced to her campaigns and her relationships with others. Theological questions were also put to her, some of them so difficult that it was thought no peasant should be able to answer them—as many theologians could not.

One of these was "Do you know if you are in the grace of God?" In the Catholic Church, this was a trick question; to answer "yes" would be considered prideful and presumptuous, while to answer "no" would be as good as a confession to sin. Joan's answer was instantaneous and without hesitation, and it surprised the entire court. "If I am not, may God place me there; if I am, may God so keep me," she responded. Her answer left her questioners speechless.

In fact, Joan often answered with a wisdom and understanding that startled the court, and her trial became an embarrassment to the

English. It could no longer be held publicly; instead, from mid-March onward, she was questioned in prison.

Now the trial began to take a turn for the worse. Although Joan did not falter, she started to realize that regardless of what she answered, she would be condemned. She started to warn the prosecutors that if they judged her poorly, God would be her protector. Delivered in her typical calm manner and with her piercing eyes, it must have been unnerving. But the judges were gaining ground, starting to find something upon which they could condemn her. They could find no evidence to charge her as a witch, but one thing was undeniable. Joan had dressed frequently as a man. In fact, standing in the court itself, she was dressed as a man as they questioned her. During that period, cross-dressing was considered a heinous crime and a sign of heresy.

As much as both Joan and the witnesses that the court questioned—among them Jean de Metz himself—argued that dressing as a man had simply been a reasonable and normal precaution, the court recognized that it had finally gotten hold of something that it could convict her for. Even though Joan protested that she was only wearing her hosen in a bid to avoid rape from her guards, the court made no attempt to defend her virginity. Instead, after weeks of trial, the court finally came to a decision. Joan was found guilty of cross-dressing. And she was sentenced to death.

Chapter 19 – The Burning of Jeanne d'Arc

"As the dog returns to his vomit," the death sentence read, "so you have returned to your errors and crimes."

Joan's calm was broken, but her conviction was not. Tears poured down her cheeks as she listened to the bishop reading her death sentence. In a moment of what she saw as weakness, she had confessed to heresy the day before, but she had quickly renounced her confession, and now it was May 30th, 1431, and she was about to be burned at the stake.

She continued to listen as the bishop read her sentence. The stake was readied, the firewood lying about its base. Eight hundred soldiers stood around her, armed to the teeth; even now, they still feared the might of Joan of Arc.

"We decree," the bishop went on, "that you are a relapsed heretic, by our present sentence which, seat in a tribunal, we utter and pronounce in this writing; we denounce you as a rotten member..."

Joan prayed quietly to herself, raising her hand to her chest to feel the tiny, hard shape of a little wooden cross that one of the English soldiers had made for her, probably from the very wood with which she was about to be burned. The shape of it reassured her a little, allowing her to stand quietly and listen to the rest of her sentence.

Then she was led to the fire. She was closely followed by Friar Martin Ladvenu, her confessor; he carried with him the crucifix from the local church, which she had begged him to bring so that she could gaze upon the face of her beloved Jesus as she burned. She wept constantly and lamented as she was bound to the stake, but she did not resist. And then, without further ado, the fire was lit beneath her. Flames licked up along the wood, roaring higher and higher, closer toward her small feet where she stood at the stake. She wore a woman's dress, but her hair was still not the usual length of the period; it tumbled, loose and dark, down her shoulders as she kept her eyes fixed resolutely on the crucifix. The flames kept rising, and as they rose, she begged Martin to lift the crucifix higher and higher. He lifted it, seeing the flames reflected in her bright blue eyes. She barely blinked, even as the smoke enveloped her.

"Jesus!" It was a scream for help or a plea for mercy—no one could say for sure, but its sheer desperation was undeniable. "Jesus!" she cried again, her tear-filled eyes still fixed on the cross. "Jesus!"

The spectators were crying; the English soldiers stood weeping as they watched Joan burn, the flames rising up to cover her body, licking at the edges of her dress, scorching up her arms and legs.

"Jesus!" Joan cried out. "Jesus!"

There was a moment of silence. Joan was hidden in the flames by now, at the very heart of the flickering blaze. Then there came one final cry. It was loud and ringing, and there was something more than fear in it. Something that could have been recognition or even joy.

"Jesus!"

And then Joan of Arc was dead.

* * * *

When the fire had died down, the English made sure to sift through the soot, looking for human ashes to prove that Joan was dead indeed, that there would be no return of France's greatest heroine. When they found her ashes, they carried them off to the River Seine, where they were tossed carelessly into the water. Floating and curling inside the waves, these little gray flakes were all that was left on earth of this bright and shining person. Her pure, high voice. Her piercing, blue eyes. Her straight posture on a horse, the ferocious determination with which she brandished her banner. It was all gone, just some gray dust now, carried off on the current of the Seine.

But Joan believed that this was not the end of the story. She believed, and she told Friar Martin, that she would be in paradise by the grace of God. She believed that she would be singing and dancing in heaven that day with the God she trusted. And after all she had suffered, after the war she didn't ask for, the treachery she had suffered, and the imprisonment that she had to endure, she still believed that the eternity she yearned for would be worth it all.

Conclusion

Illustration IX: Statue to Joan of Arc, Paris

In the years following the death of Joan of Arc, Charles VII would continue to rule over France, and he grew into an able king who established one of the first standing armies in the medieval world.

This move would not only sound the first death knell of the age of chivalry, which would eventually bring an end to the Dark Ages, but it also finished off his victory over England in the Hundred Years' War. Two decades after Joan died, the war would be over. France won a decisive victory, and the English were driven back to Great Britain, forced out of the borders of France for good in 1453.

Joan's name still remained on every pair of lips in the kingdom, even though her ashes had long since dissolved into the Seine. While the war was won by good military command during the later years of Charles's reign, no one could deny then—or can deny now—that the appearance of Joan of Arc brought about what could be considered a miraculous change in the war. Before she arrived at Chinon, France was undoubtedly losing the war; to the English and to Charles himself, it seemed to be only a matter of time before France would be lost. Yet France didn't lose. It won the war, and it only started winning when a strange teenage peasant girl arrived in the court of the king and convinced him that God had sent her to save his country.

Despite the fact that Joan remains one of the most well-studied figures from the Middle Ages, scientists still have not been able to pinpoint a cause for her visions. Whatever their cause, they made her one of the most legendary figures in France, a symbol of the country's national identity, and one of the first warrior women who would begin to turn the tide in a world dominated by men.

In 1452, long after her death but before the war had officially ended, Joan's mother requested a retrial. She knew full well that her daughter had died unfairly, and she couldn't bear to see Joan go down in history as a heretic. Pope Calixtus III agreed to the trial, and after three years of investigation, Joan's name was cleared in 1456. Instead, the bishop that had judged her, Pierre Cauchon, was found guilty of heresy himself for persecuting her due to his political agenda.

In the years that followed, multiple statues and other monuments were erected to Joan. Some of the places that played a key role in her life—such as her birthplace and the tower in Rouen where she was imprisoned—are still in existence and have become major tourist attractions. Statues to her stand in Paris and Orléans, among others. Multiple books and movies have been made about her, including one famous biography by Mark Twain.

Joan has also been the subject of some interesting theories, some of which celebrate her as a genius, others calling her either mad, pagan, or simply a myth. One thing that remains certain is that Joan is a mysterious figure, and many questions about her life still go unanswered by history and science. To the Christian faith, she is a symbol of what God can do through small and ordinary people.

This fact would be demonstrated a little more than a hundred years ago when Joan was officially canonized in 1909—497 years after she was born. She became known as Saint Joan, the patron saint of France. Now, a feast day has been dedicated to her, as well as a national holiday; rallying songs in the First World War mentioned her and spoke of her story, and even today, she remains a symbol of hope and inspiration.

Still, there is something a little tragic about Joan's story. In her own words, she had never asked to be a warrior maiden. All she wanted was a simple, ordinary life spinning wool in boring little Domrémy. Instead, she had to endure battles and betrayal, trials and execution, treachery and doubt. She would die a horrible, painful martyr's death at the tender age of only nineteen, condemned by the very church that she served so fervently. And yet, according to Joan, she had known what was coming. She had walked into her own death with open eyes, driven by her passionate devotion to her faith and to France.

Joan was many things: mysterious, determined, enigmatic, faithful, and undoubtedly a little bit strange. One thing, however, stands out throughout her story, running through the tapestry of her life like a golden thread. In a war that had been started by greed, when a power-hungry king decided that one kingdom was simply not enough, Joan's actions are marked by unselfishness. Over and over again, she chose a course that often resulted in pain and unhappiness for herself. If she hadn't, France might have never won the war. And history would look very, very different.

Here's another book by Captivating History that you might be interested in

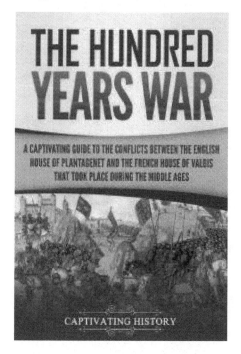

And another one…

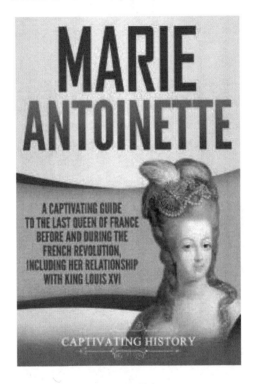

Free Bonus from Captivating History (Available for a Limited time)

Hi History Lovers!

Now you have a chance to join our exclusive history list so you can get your first history ebook for free as well as discounts and a potential to get more history books for free! Simply visit the link below to join.

Captivatinghistory.com/ebook

Also, make sure to follow us on Facebook, Twitter and Youtube by searching for Captivating History.

Sources

The Hundred Years' War: A Captivating Guide to the Conflicts Between the English House of Plantagenet and the French House of Valois That Took Place During the Middle Ages, by Captivating History, 2018

https://en.wikipedia.org/wiki/Bede

https://www.jeanne-darc.info/biography/prophecies/

https://en.wikipedia.org/wiki/Hundred_Years'_War

Illustration I: By Arnaud 25 - Own work, CC BY-SA 4.0, https://commons.wikimedia.org/w/index.php?curid=53420390

https://en.wikipedia.org/wiki/Bible_translations_into_French#Chronological_list

https://www.historytoday.com/richard-cavendish/joan-arc-born-domr%C3%A9my

https://sites.google.com/site/byuhistory201group6/group-project/the-lancastrian-phase

https://en.wikipedia.org/wiki/Treaty_of_Troyes

https://www.encyclopedia.com/history/modern-europe/treaties-and-alliances/treaty-troyes

http://movies2.nytimes.com/books/first/g/gordon-joan.html

https://en.wikipedia.org/wiki/Charles_VI_of_France#English_invasion_and_death

https://en.wikipedia.org/wiki/Henry_VI_of_England

https://www.jeanne-darc.info/biography/visions/

https://www.thoughtco.com/medieval-child-teens-at-work-and-play-1789126

https://en.wikipedia.org/wiki/Catherine_of_Alexandria

https://en.wikipedia.org/wiki/Margaret_the_Virgin

https://injoanofarcsfootsteps.com/articles/tag/robert-de-baudricourt/

https://en.wikipedia.org/wiki/Robert_de_Baudricourt

Illustration II: By The Life of Joan of Arc, Vol. 1 and 2, Anatole France ; http://www.gutenberg.org/etext/19488, Public Domain, https://commons.wikimedia.org/w/index.php?curid=1553037

http://www.maidofheaven.com/joanofarc_vaucouleurs.asp

https://en.wikipedia.org/wiki/Battle_of_the_Herrings

https://www.stewartsociety.org/history-of-the-stewarts.cfm?section=battles-and-historical-events&subcatid=1&histid=506

https://en.wikipedia.org/wiki/Charles_VII_of_France#King_of_Bourges

https://medium.com/interesting-histories/interesting-histories-joan-of-arc-7512922e41d0

Illustration III: By Andrew C.P. Haggard (1854–1923)modified and colorized by Rinaldum - original source: Andrew C.P. Haggard: France of Joan of Arc New York John Lane Company 1912transferred to Commons from fr:Image:Portrait jeanne d'arc.jpg, which was taken from lib.utexas.edu (original image source was here, archived version), Public Domain, https://commons.wikimedia.org/w/index.php?curid=94591

http://www.maidofheaven.com/joanofarc_quote_I_am_not_afraid.asp

https://www.jeanne-darc.info/trials-index/the-examination-at-poitiers/

http://www.indiana.edu/~dmdhist/joan.htm

http://archive.joan-of-arc.org/joanofarc_short_biography.html

Illustration IV: By Jules Eugène Lenepveu (1819 – 1898) - published on en.wiki here by User:Gdr, taken from http://194.165.231.32/hemma/mathias/jeannedarc/lenepveu2.jpg, Public Domain, https://commons.wikimedia.org/w/index.php?curid=803067

https://en.wikipedia.org/wiki/Siege_of_Orl%C3%A9ans#Assault_on_the_Tourelles_2

https://www.thoughtco.com/hundred-years-war-siege-of-orleans-2360758

http://www.joan-of-arc.org/joanofarc_life_summary_orleans2.html

https://www.history.com/topics/middle-ages/siege-of-orleans

http://www.joan-of-arc.org/joanofarc_life_summary_victoire.html

http://www.maidofheaven.com/joanofarc_patay_battle.asp

https://www.thoughtco.com/hundred-years-war-battle-of-patay-2360756

https://www.sparknotes.com/biography/joanofarc/section5/

Illustration V:
https://commons.wikimedia.org/wiki/File:Troyes_Rue_Linard_Gonthier_R01.jpg

http://joan-of-arc.org/joanofarc_life_summary_rheims.html

https://www.cs.mcgill.ca/~rwest/wikispeedia/wpcd/wp/j/Joan_of_Arc.htm

Illustration VI:
https://en.wikipedia.org/wiki/Joan_of_Arc_at_the_Coronation_of_Charles_VII

http://www.maidofheaven.com/joanofarc_reims_coronation.asp

https://en.wikipedia.org/wiki/Reims_Cathedral

http://jean-claude.colrat.pagesperso-orange.fr/2-sacre.htm

Illustration VII:

By Anonymous - This image comes from Gallica Digital Library and is available under the digital ID btv1b105380390/f144, Public Domain, https://commons.wikimedia.org/w/index.php?curid=16973390

https://www.catholic.org/saints/saint.php?saint_id=120

http://www.maidofheaven.com/joanofarc_paris.asp

https://www.sparknotes.com/biography/joanofarc/section7/

https://www.revolvy.com/page/Siege-of-Paris-%281429%29

https://www.jeanne-darc.info/battles-of-jeanne-darc/attack-on-paris-1429/

http://www.maidofheaven.com/joanofarc_jeanne_darc_autumn_1429.asp

http://www.maidofheaven.com/joanofarc_long_biography.asp

https://en.wikipedia.org/wiki/Hundred_Years'_War_%281415%E2%80%9353%29#The_Anglo-Burgundian_alliance_leads_to_the_Treaty_of_Troyes

https://en.wikipedia.org/wiki/Siege_of_Saint-Pierre-le-Mo%C3%BBtier

http://www.maidofheaven.com/marktwain/joanofarc_mark_twain_personal_recollections_book2_chapter41.asp#compiegne

https://www.jeanne-darc.info/battles-of-jeanne-darc/siege-of-compiegne/

Illustration VIII: By Paul Delaroche - [1], Public Domain, https://commons.wikimedia.org/w/index.php?curid=27221

http://www.stjoan-center.com/time_line/part08.html

http://www.maidofheaven.com/joanofarc_maidoffrance_captivity.asp

https://history.howstuffworks.com/history-vs-myth/joan-of-arc-trial2.htm

https://www.jeanne-darc.info/trial-of-condemnation-index/

https://sourcebooks.fordham.edu/basis/joanofarc-trial.asp

https://en.wikipedia.org/wiki/Trial_of_Joan_of_Arc#Preliminary_inquiry

http://www.maidofheaven.com/joanofarc_feastday.asp

http://www.maidofheaven.com/joanofarc_death_sentence.asp

https://en.wikipedia.org/wiki/Joan_of_Arc

https://en.wikipedia.org/wiki/Death_by_burning#Christian_states

Illustration IX: https://commons.wikimedia.org/wiki/File:Joan_of_Arc_Emmanuel_Fremiet.jpg